Nature of Matter

Grades 5-8

Written by Lars Rose and Heidrun Spohr
Illustrated by S&S Learning Materials

About the authors

Lars Rose, M.Sc., is an award winning scientist researching for his PhD in alternative energy technology at the University of British Columbia (UBC) and the National Research Council. He coordinates university students for the national science outreach program Let's Talk Science, and regularly gives alternative energy and science presentations to a wide variety of organizations and audiences of all ages and backgrounds. He is a highly experienced science writer and teaches science and engineering in grades K-12 throughout Canada.

Heidrun Spohr, M.Chem., graduated from the University of Bath, UK and is doing research for her PhD in Chemistry at UBC. She has more than six years experience teaching undergraduate students in Europe and Canada. She teaches science to elementary and secondary classrooms on a volunteer basis and is a leadership advocate for propagating the proper Scientific Method to her students.

Both hail from the city after which element 110 (Darmstadtium) has been named.

ISBN 978-1-55495-020-1
Copyright 2009

Published in the U.S.A by:
On The Mark Press
3909 Witmer Road PMB 175
Niagara Falls, New York
14305
www.onthemarkpress.com

Published in Canada by:
S&S Learning Materials
15 Dairy Avenue
Napanee, Ontario
K7R 1M4
www.sslearning.com

Permission to Reproduce

Permission is granted to the individual teacher who purchases one copy of this book to reproduce the student activity material for use in his/her classroom only. Reproduction of these materials for an entire school or for a school system, or for other colleagues or for commercial sale is **strictly prohibited**. No part of this publication may be transmitted in any form or by any means, electronic, mechanical, recording or otherwise without the prior written permission of the publisher. "We acknowledge the financial support of the Government of Canada through the Book Publishing Industry Development Program (BPIDP) for this project." Printed in Canada. All Rights Reserved

At A Glance

Learning Expectations

	Skills Activities	Physical Science	Social Science	Review of Changes of Matter	External Influences	Physical Changes	Chemical Changes	Mixtures and Solutions
Language Skills								
Reading and listening comprehension	•	•	•	•	•	•	•	•
Communicating in writing	•	•	•	•	•	•	•	•
Vocabulary development	•	•	•	•	•	•	•	•
Creating reports	•	•	•	•	•	•	•	•
Critical Thinking and Reasoning								
Generating questions		•	•	•	•	•	•	•
Developing research skills and show an understanding of the scientific method		•		•	•	•	•	•
Recording, observation, comparison, and critical analysis of data	•	•	•	•	•	•	•	•
Applying acquired knowledge	•	•	•	•	•	•	•	•
Self-evaluation	•	•	•	•	•	•	•	•
Physical and Scientific Skills								
Conduct investigations into States of Matter	•	•		•	•	•	•	•
Describe the Particle Theory of matter and use it to explain changes of state	•	•		•	•	•	•	•
Show understanding of external influences on matter	•			•	•			
Show thorough understanding of the relationships and origins of different scientific scales (temperature, pressure)		•			•			
Describe the distinction between pure substances and mixtures		•				•	•	•
Identify factors that affect solubility and describe, through observation, solution concentration	•	•				•	•	•
Describe liquids in terms of their viscosity, density, flow rate, buoyancy		•			•	•		
Describe qualitatively the relationship between mass, volume, weight, density	•		•		•			
Classify a variety of substances used in daily life as pure substances, solutions, or mechanical mixtures		•		•				•
Describe common chemical changes in terms of properties of reactants and products		•					•	•
Show a thorough understanding of the environmental impact of human actions	•	•	•				•	•
Explain why mass is conserved in physical and chemical changes		•			•	•	•	
Demonstrate the effects of heating and cooling on the volume of solids, liquids, and gases, and give examples from daily life	•	•	•	•	•			
Compare the boiling and melting points of a variety of substances and recognize that boiling and melting points are properties of pure substances and dependent on external actors		•		•	•			•
Identify materials that are good heat insulators and good heat conductors		•			•	•		
Realize that pure substances are made up of one type of particle and that mixtures are made up of more types		•		•	•			•

Table of Contents

At a Glance	2
Teacher Assessment Rubric	4
Student Assessment Rubric	6
Introduction	8
Materials List	9
Introduction to Experimentation	10
Introduction to Experimentation Student Sheet	12
Matter Dictionary	13
Teacher Notes: Review of the States of Matter	15
Matter Matters: What's the Matter?	17
Matter Matters: Matter Around You	18
Classify With Class!	20
Teacher Notes: Introduction of Matter - Properties and External Influences	21
Let's Get Some Heat!	22
Hot Calculations	23
The Pressure	24
Pressure Worksheet	25
Rise and Shine	26
Rise and Shine Worksheet	27
The Matter Game	28
The Matter Game Worksheet	29
That's Massive!: Mass, Volume, Density (Why Do Ships Swim?)	30
Oily Icing	32
Just Hot Gas: External Influence of Temperature on Gaseous Matter	33
Just Hot Gas Worksheet	34
Press It!: External Influence of Pressure on Density (Compressibility)	35
The Swirl of Hot Color: Influence of Temperature on Solid and Liquid Matter	36
The Swirl of Hot Color Worksheet	37
Some Honey, Honey?: Viscosity Experiments	38
Some Honey, Honey?: Viscosity Experiments Worksheets 1 & 2	40
Teacher Notes: Matter Changes in the Classroom – Physical Changes	42
Let's Get Changed: Exchanges Between States	43
Let's Get Changed: Exchanges Between States Worksheet	44
Creating Clouds 1	45
Creating Clouds 2	46
Creating Clouds 1 and 2 Worksheet	47
The Cloud Game	48
The Cloud Game Worksheet	49
Slightly Sublime	50
Slightly Sublime Worksheet	51
CO_2 Fun	52
CO_2 Fun Worksheet	54
Making a Fire Extinguisher	56
Crystal, Crystal on the Wall	57
Teacher Notes: Matter Changes in the Classroom – Chemical Changes	59
Chemical Creation of Gases and Heat	60
Chemical Creation of Gases and Heat Worksheet	61
React-it	62
React-it Worksheet	63
Black Sugar Snake 1	64
Black Sugar Snake 2	65
Matter Waste: Environmental Impacts of Reactions	66
Teacher Notes: Mixtures and Solutions	67
Mix It, Shake It, Separate It: An Introduction to Miscibility	68
Mix It, Shake It, Separate It Worksheet	69
Solu-What?: An Introduction of Solute/Solubility/Concentration & Sugar-Gro'	70
Solu-What? Worksheet	71
Solu-Solubility - a poem	73
Dio-mio-Iodine	74
Dio-mio-Iodine Solvent – Solubility Worksheet	75
They Live in the Jungle	76
Do-It-Yourself Precious Gemstones	78
Tensing Surfaces: Liquid/Gas Interfaces	81
Un-tensing Surfaces	82
Bubble-icious	83
Mixing Oil and Water: Liquid/Liquid Interfaces	84
Muddy Hell: The Science of Soil Erosion: Liquid/Solid Mixtures	85
Muddy Hell Worksheet	86
A Little Fizz to Freeze: Liquid/Gas Mixtures	87
Smoking Mirrors: Gas/Solid Mixtures	88
The Needle in the Haystack: How to Separate Mixtures	89
The Needle in the Haystack Worksheet	90
Answer Key	91

Teacher Assessment Rubric

Student's Name: _____

Criteria	Level 1	Level 2	Level 3	Level 4
Understanding of basic concepts relating to the nature of matter	Demonstrates limited understanding of what constitutes matter	Demonstrates some understanding of what constitutes matter	Demonstrates considerable understanding of what constitutes matter	Demonstrates thorough and insightful understanding of what constitutes matter
Investigation of external factors that affect changes in the state of matter	Demonstrates limited ability to determine external factors that affect changes in the state of matter Follows few safety procedures and rules	Demonstrates some ability to determine external factors that affect changes in the state of matter Follows some safety procedures and rules	Demonstrates considerable ability to determine external factors that affect changes in the state of matter Follows most safety procedures and rules	Demonstrates superior ability to determine external factors that affect changes in the state of matter Follows all safety procedures and rules
Communication of required knowledge	Communicates results of investigation ineffectively Makes limited use of correct science and technology vocabulary Demonstrates limited organization in written work including use of labeled tables, charts and diagrams	Communicates results of investigation somewhat effectively Makes some use of correct science and technology vocabulary Demonstrates some organization in written work including use of labeled tables, charts and diagrams	Communicates results of investigation effectively Makes good use of correct science and technology vocabulary Demonstrates good organization in written work including use of labeled tables, charts and diagrams	Communicates results of investigation highly effectively Makes excellent use of correct science and technology vocabulary Demonstrates excellent and careful organization in written work including use of labeled tables, charts and diagrams

Teacher Group Work Assesment Rubric

Group Work Rubric Name: _____

	Possible Points	Points Earned	
		Student	Teacher
The student was prepared for the group work.			
The student completes all individual tasks for the group on time.			
The student completes all individual tasks for the group correctly and with high quality.			
The student participates in the group in a constructive way.			
The student shares the responsibility of helping the group get the assignment completed according to the given directions.			

_____
_____
_____
_____
_____

Group Work Rubric Name: _____

	Possible Points	Points Earned	
		Student	Teacher
The student was prepared for the group work.			
The student completes all individual tasks for the group on time.			
The student completes all individual tasks for the group correctly and with high quality.			
The student participates in the group in a constructive way.			
The student shares the responsibility of helping the group get the assignment completed according to the given directions.			

_____
_____
_____
_____
_____

Student Self-Assessment Rubric

Independent Investigation Rubric   Name: _____

Question	
The question is clear and well-focused.	4
The question is relatively clear and focused.	3
The question is incomplete and unclear.	2
There is no question.	1
I give myself	
My teacher gives me	
Planning	
There was a clear, well-developed plan organized by the student which includes the question, materials, procedure, and safety.	4
There was a plan, but some assistance from the teacher was required.	3
There are steps missing from the plan, teacher organized what the student needed to do.	2
There was no plan organized by the student.	1
I give myself	
My teacher gives me	
Carrying Out the Investigation	
All materials are used safely, appropriately and ethically following learned procedures.	4
Most materials are used safely, appropriately and ethically following learned procedures.	3
Some materials are used safely, appropriately and ethically and learned procedure is not always followed.	2
Materials are not used safely, appropriately or ethically and learned procedures are not followed.	1
I give myself	
My teacher gives me	
Reporting	
Complete report includes observations and data recorded to clearly answer the question with detail, accuracy and understanding.	4
Complete report includes observations and data recorded to answer the question with some detail.	3
Incomplete report which used some of the observations and only answered part of the question.	2
Incomplete report with missing details which did not answer the question.	1
I give myself	
My teacher gives me	

Additional comments:_____

_____

_____

Student Self-Assessment Rubric

Student Effort Rubric   Name: _____

- **4** I worked on the task with maximum effort.
- **3** I worked on the task but stopped early.
- **2** I worked on the task for a while but put very little effort into it.
- **1** I did not even start the task.

Activity/Investigation																				
Score																				

Student Achievement Rubric   Name: _____

- **3** I met all of the objectives of the activity or investigation.
- **2** I met some of the objectives of the activity or investigation but did not meet others.
- **1** I did not meet the objectives of the activity or investigation.
- **0** I did not turn in the assignment.

Activity/Investigation																				
Score																				

Introduction

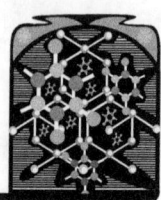

Matter is all around us. Matter is what we are. Matter is what we smell, breathe, see, hear, taste, and feel. Understanding matter means understanding the universe we live in. The core of understanding phases of matter is to understand Particle Theory. This theory and its many versatile applications are explained in this book. The subject is broken down into bite-sized activities that can be performed in a classroom setting as well as by students at home. Some are quick experiments; others include observations over many weeks. All are unified by explaining how matter interacts with other matter, how phases are changed by external influences, and how all that matter matters to us.

The book starts with a review of the three states of matter (well four, if one includes plasmas and five including Bose-Einstein condensates). It then continues to give ample opportunity for experimentation with the behavior of matter towards external influences. The influence of temperature and pressure on the states of matter can be experienced in a variety of hands-on experiments. It will become clear that both pressure and temperature of a substance are dependent on each other, and a state cannot be clearly defined without knowing both.

Furthermore, physical and chemical changes are elaborated. The experiments include the visualization of changes of matter, beginning with the well-known system of water and moving towards material systems that lack some of the states under atmospheric conditions. Furthermore, the chemical production of gases from solids, the visible changes in metals during oxidation and corrosion, and the growth of solid crystals from solutions can be experienced.

Finally, the book includes curricular activities on separating matter. The processes simplified here are the foundation upon which our materials production from raw resources is based and is thus vital to the level of technology we have obtained. The experiments go from understanding the differences in matter to harnessing that knowledge into useful separation methods. The book thus comes full circle in explaining the science and marvel there is to matter in our universe.

Notes to the Teacher:

- Plan the activities based on your curriculum requirements. Many substitutions can be made to allow the students to focus on local climate and other issues in order to meet curriculum requirements.

- Collect materials well in advance of doing activities and investigations.

- If you are not familiar with the use and care of some of the setups described in this book, try to go through the activity yourself before the students begin that activity in this book.

- Discuss and practice safety procedures before doing any new activities or using unfamiliar equipment.

- Time permitting, encourage the students to do the extensions in the activities and investigations, many of which are cross-curricular. These ideas show how knowledge in the field of matter can cross subject boundaries and enhance the students' perception of the world.

Materials List

Review of the Three, Four, Five? States of Matter:

Balloons, earth, water, chalk, soap
<u>Extensions</u>: desks, coins, pencils, buildings, windows, snowflakes, copper, iron, wood, plastic, styrofoam, alcohol, milk, juice, helium, water vapor

Introduction of Matter Properties and External Influences:

Wood (varying sizes and shapes), wire, tin can, screws, nails, glue, cable binders, hot glue, hammer, screw driver, drill, balance, angle brackets, solder, cable binders, pressurized glass containers, vacuum tubes, hot plate, thermometer, masking tape, Erlenmeyers/beakers, tap water, test tubes, rubber stopper, graduated cylinder, vegetable oil, colored ice cubes, boiling water, ice cold water, hair dryer, microwave, empty plastic bottle, large container, syringe, straw, cups, ice cream, glass marbles, honey, vegetable oil, stop watch, letter sized mat, weight, force meter

Matter Changes in the Classroom: Physical Changes

Isopropanol, water, thick-walled Erlenmeyer flask, beaker, rubber stopper with hole, hollow glass tubes, polymer hose, air pump, matches, masking tape, colored head bands, hats, caps, towel, cloth, balance, freezer, dry ice, ice cubes, detergent, straws, thermometer, hot plate, Bunsen burner, laboratory glassware, overhead projector, tongs, heat protection gloves, Petri dish, thymol, oven, candle, tea light

Matter Changes in the Classroom: Chemical Changes

Large bowl, small dish, baking soda, candle, match, lighter, vinegar, Erlenmeyer flask or beaker, hydrogen peroxide, manganese dioxide, balloon, spoon, nails, transparent beakers, grease, de-ionized water, paint, salt, clinging foil, bucket, stone, sulfuric acid, sugar, fume hood, lab coat, safety glasses, gloves, safety equipment, sand, alcohol, lighter fluid, baking soda, icing sugar

Mixtures and Solutions:

Just for discussion (not the actual samples): milk, smoke, clouds, pop, blood, tar sand.
<u>Experimental equipment</u>: clear glass beaker, jam glass, paper clip, water, salt, sugar, thread, chopstick, hot plate, carbon tetrachloride (can be replaced with toluene or cyclohexane or other chemicals), fume hood, proper safety equipment, ether, graduated cylinder, iodine, sodium silicate, distilled water, small jars or vials, lids, washed sand, various metal salts (for example: aluminum chloride, copper chloride, aluminum nitrate, copper sulfate, aluminum potassium sulfate, iron chloride, chromium chloride, iron sulfate, chromium nitrate, nickel chloride, cobalt chloride, nickel sulfate, cobalt nitrate, tin chloride), egg shell, clam shell, marble, copper sulfate, large open glass, metal wire, woolen thread, chopstick, nail polish remover, tweezers, soap, dish detergent, plastic or ceramic dishes, plates, cups, tap water, paper, ballpoint pen, juice, ethanol, glue, pipe cleaner, straw, vegetable oil, cups, aluminum roasting pan, soil, timer, Bunsen burner, candle, ceramic plate, carbonated drink, bowl full of ice, table salt, thermometer, sieve, sugar, chalk, tea leaves, marble, nails, sand, styrofoam granules, soap, flower, bathing salt, magnets, tweezers, dish detergent, plastic or ceramic dishes, plates, cups, toothbrush, magnifying glass, food coloring, coffee filter

Introduction to Experimentation

"How to do Science" in Everyday Classrooms as well as Science Fairs.

Definitions:

Experiment: An experiment is an investigation undertaken to test a specific hypothesis. Experimental variables are to be identified and controlled during experimentation.

Study: A study is a collection and analysis of data to reveal the evidence of a fact of scientific interest. Depending on the interest of a student, it could include a study of cause and effect relationships or theoretical investigations of scientific data, for example from reliable (peer review) literature. The internet cannot be treated as a reliable source.

Invention: The students develop a heretofore unknown material, process or device (hardware/software), conduct literature research proving that the idea is new and potentially patentable, and evaluate their ideas.

The Process of Setting Up an Experiment: The following text outlines a potential process of designing and executing an experiment in a proper scientific manner. Obviously, not all the steps might be relevant to each student's experimentation; however, the principle layout usually remains the same. All these points apply to the classroom as well as other science activities such as science fairs.

Important Issues:

What are the students interested in? Is this an original idea, at least unique to the school? Is the scope of the project reasonable, and doable within a limited amount of time and resources? Will the students be able to access the necessary equipment/supplies?

So what to do:

a) **Identify the Scientific Problems:** Coming up with an original and feasible idea for an experiment can be very difficult for students. However, this book might give some ideas to draw from for experimentations. Also, the internet is a vast resource to draw from for designing proper science experiments. However, the information is not necessarily correct, since the internet as a whole is not scientifically peer-reviewed. This point should be strongly emphasized with the students. Government or university sites often have better content than companies which are intent on selling their products. Even open-source based sites such as Wikipedia might give out wrong information.

b) **Make Observations and Perform Background Research:** Every scientist needs to do background research prior to starting a project. This is no different for classroom projects. Students should be encouraged to talk to teachers, parents, and friends, maybe even find scientists in the field and contact them, in order to learn more about their topic and to help narrow down the scope of a project. Libraries are also a good source to find reputable books on all manner of topics.

c) **Form Hypotheses:** Most students will learn in class what a hypothesis is. A hypothesis is an educated guess about the answer to their question, based on observations and information that has been collected about the project. It is only a tentative explanation for something that has to be founded by further investigation. Often times, students revise their hypothesis after they found a different explanation due to experimentation. This should be discouraged, since a hypothesis is just that. A hypothesis, and not a conclusion. Science experiments that give sound reasons for opposing a hypothesis often offer strong, sound research results.

d) **Design an Experiment:** Based on the hypotheses, experiments will have to be designed to test the tentative explanations given. The fewer variables are tested for, the clearer will the outcome be. Also, the experiment must not be biased towards a particular outcome in advance. Experiment variation, result precision and control, and the ideas of dependent and independent variables should be clear before starting. For science fairs, students should keep their projects innovative. There are three critical principles to emphasize and the students should understand why they are so important:

Controls – all variables other than the independent variable (i.e., the variable being tested) are kept the same for the control and experimental groups

Replication – sufficient numbers of test subjects in both control and experimental groups

Randomization – should be done wherever and whenever possible! The experiment should not be influenced by biases. For example, if a coin is flipped, multiple coins should be used to randomize the results. Or, if water tests are made, they have to be made in different areas in different depths.

Make Observations and Record Results: When the time comes to actually conduct the experiment, the students should be encouraged to take notes very carefully. Observing involves recording and taking notes of all outcomes of experiments. The experiments must be reproducible and everything done has to be recorded minutely.

f) **Analyze Results:** During and after data recording, the students need to analyze their results. This step involves organizing the observations and deciding if those observations say something about the question/problem. Did the experiment give the expected results? Was the experiment performed with the exact same steps each time? Are there other causes that were not considered or observed? Were there errors in the observations? The topic of simple statistical analysis, precision, and accuracy can be introduced at this point.

g) **Create Defendable Conclusions:** Students should use the analysis of their observations to make conclusions about their experiment. There are two possible conclusions: either the experiment supported the hypothesis or it did not support the hypothesis. It is totally fine for a hypothesis to not be supported by the experimental results. However, it is important to express why that might be the case. Would another further experiment be valuable? The student should think about how the conclusion fits into the background information they have found.

Let's Do The Scientific Method

Introduction to Experimentation for Students:

The Scientific Method is an easy guide to get your experiments right. You can use this page for all your experiments.

Investigate
1. Consider a question to investigate.
   _____
   _____

Predict
2. Predict what you think will happen (hypothesize).
   _____
   _____

Plan
3. Create a detailed procedure of how you plan to investigate your question.
   _____
   _____
   _____
   _____

Observe
4. Record all observations. Record everything you do. Never eradicate your data. If something is wrong, only cross it out so it is still legible. You might require the information at a later point.
   _____
   _____
   _____

Conclude
5. Write a conclusion. This should be based on your observation. It does not have to coincide with your prediction.
   _____
   _____
   _____
   _____

Matter Dictionary

Allotrope: Allotropy is the property of some chemical elements which can occur in more than one crystal structure. The atoms are arranged differently by chemical bonds. The forms are known as allotropes of that element.

Anion: Negatively charged ion. Usually a non-metal ion.

Cation: Positively charged ion. Usually a metal ion.

Chaos: Not the natural state of a classroom, but a state of things in which chance is supreme. The confused, unorganized state of primordial matter before the creation of distinct forms.

Colloid: A mixture where one substance is dispersed evenly throughout another. Some colloids may appear to be solutions but are in fact not. A colloidal system consists of two separate phases: a dispersed phase or internal phase and a continuous phase or dispersion medium. A colloidal system may be of any state: solid, liquid or gas.

Compressibility: Compressibility is a measure of the relative volume change of matter as a response to a pressure change.

Concentration: A measure of the amount of one component (solute) with respect to a host material (solvent). 0% denotes no presence of the component. 100% denotes no presence of the host material.

Conductivity: Describes the ease with which one material diffuses through another material. It is most often used for electron flow within materials (electric conductivity). Can be applied to any number of phenomena such as thermal heat transfer, ionic conductivity, diffusion, etc.

Density: Density generally describes the distribution of unit mass per unit volume.

Electron: Fundamental subatomic particle. Carries a negative electric charge.

Equilibrium: Matter in equilibrium does not change with time. An external force has to be applied to change matter that is in equilibrium. While the force works, it is no longer in equilibrium.

Force: In physics, force is strength or energy exerted or brought to bear. It is the cause of motion changes and may be experienced as a twist, a push or a pull.

Gas: A gas is one of the states of matter. It consists of a collection of particles without a definite shape or volume that are in more or less random (chaotic) motion. This is also the origin of the source term for gas, an alteration of the Latin word "chaos".

Hardness: Hardness refers to various properties of matter in the solid state that give it high resistance to various kinds of shape change when force is applied. Should never be confused with toughness.

Insoluble: A solute not capable of being dissolved in the solvent.

Ion: An ion can be an atom or molecule. It has lost or gained one or more (valence) electrons. It is thus electrically charged. The charge can be positive (see cation) or negative (see anion).

Liquid: A liquid is a fluid that has weak interactions between its molecules. The particles are loosely arranged. They follow the shape of their container.

Osmosis: Tendency of liquids to passively diffuse through a porous membrane or partition that separates them.

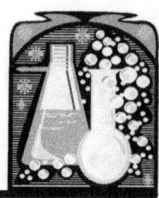

Matter Dictionary

Pressure: A force applied over a unit area. If you think of air, think of one square meter of ground. Imagine that all air molecules above that square meter press down on it with a certain (measurable) force.

Property: Quality or trait belonging and especially peculiar to an individual or thing.

Shape: The outer appearance of an object.

Solid: A solid contains atoms or molecules that are packed closely together in fixed positions in space relative to each other.

Solubility: Solubility shows the ability for a substance, the solute, to dissolve in a solvent. It is measured in terms of the maximum amount of solute dissolved in a solvent at equilibrium.

Solute: A substance dissolved in a host material (solvent).

Solution: A solution is a homogeneous mixture composed of more than one substance. In such a mixture, a solute is dissolved in another substance, known as a solvent. According to the particle theory, particles have an attraction for each other. The attraction between the particles of solute and solvent keeps them in solution.

Solvent: Denotation for the host material in a solution (see solution or concentration).

Stalagmites: A cone of carbonate or lime which gradually forms a column starting from ground level.

Stalactites: A cone of carbonate slowly forming a column starting from a ceiling.

State: A state describes what properties a certain type of matter has under given pressure and temperature conditions.

Surfactant/Tenside: Surface-active chemical (surfactant). Substance added to a material in order to reduce its surface tension with respect to a different material. This increases its wetting or spreading properties on this other material. Detergents are tensides.

Temperature: Temperature is one of the principal parameters of thermodynamics. On the microscopic scale, temperature is defined as the average energy of microscopic motions of particles. On the macroscopic scale, temperature is the unique physical property that determines the direction of heat flow between two objects placed in thermal contact. If no net heat flow occurs, the two objects have the same temperature. Otherwise heat flows from the hotter object to the colder object.

Toughness: Toughness is the resistance to fracture of a material when stressed. It is defined as the amount of energy per volume that a material can absorb before rupturing.

Transition: The change of state due to external influence.

Valence: An atom often contains many shells of electrons. Electrons can only be in a certain shell. Just think of the rings of Saturn as a comparison. Valence electrons are the electrons contained in the outermost electron shell of an atom. The outermost electron shell of an atom is called the "valence" shell.

Viscosity: Viscosity is the opposite of liquidity, and describes the resistance of a fluid to being deformed (including flow).

Volume: The amount of space occupied by a three-dimensional object as measured in cubic units.

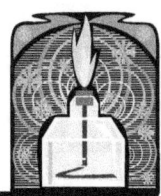

Teacher Notes

Review of the Three, Four, Five States of Matter

The essential core of understanding phases of matter is to understand the particle theory, which is summarized below. The primary step towards understanding the particle theory is to recognize that all matter is made up of smaller parts, the "particles." The particle theory is about how all the "stuff" in the universe is organized in smaller and smaller parts. Science and technology are still discovering smaller and smaller components of matter. However, these often esoteric subatomic theories will not be part of these books. They are definitely worth a quick read on the Internet.

Matter and Phases

Everything in the universe can be classified as either matter or energy. Matter is the term used to describe "things that are". The definition of matter is that it has mass and takes up space. All "stuff" is made up of atoms (and atoms are made from even smaller "stuff"), and all atoms are matter. Matter is best explained and understood in terms of the particle theory. There are currently 117 (111 of which are officially named) different types of atoms (elements). For the purpose of Grade 5-8 science classes, these atoms cannot be broken down further and can be treated as solid spheres. Each atom varies in the number of subatomic particles it contains in its center core. As our understanding of science increases, we increase the number of known subatomic particles beyond the dozens, but the basics are protons and neutrons in the center of the atom, and electrons whirling around the core. Other, even smaller subatomic particles whose names you might hear mentioned include: quarks and gluons, which make up protons and neutrons. Photons and neutrinos are two other subatomic particles.

All of the matter on Earth is made up of those 117 elements. In nature, virtually all atoms are found combined in a variety of ways with other atoms. These larger particles are called molecules; molecules are the basis of all matter and materials. It is the properties of molecules that give matter and materials their properties. Some elements are found in a very pure state. Gold is one of these; oxygen is another. This does not mean, however, that oxygen atoms are found singly. Oxygen atoms join with another oxygen atom. The oxygen molecule, the state in which oxygen is normally found, thus has two oxygen atoms. Ozone is three oxygen atoms bound together. Also it should be mentioned that even very pure gold is always alloyed with other atoms such as silver or platinum. And oxygen makes up only one fifth of our atmosphere.

If two different kinds of elements are combined in a molecule, it is called a compound. Water is a compound. It contains two hydrogen atoms and one oxygen atom. Organic compounds are those associated with living things. All life on our planet is composed of molecules containing the element carbon. Organic compounds then, contain carbon. Organic molecules are among the largest molecules and may contain thousands of atoms. DNA, proteins, and sugars are all organic compounds. Inorganic compounds are not associated with the building blocks of life, and are not usually found in living things. Ozone, carbon dioxide, and sodium chloride (table salt) are examples of inorganic compounds.

Teacher Notes

Review of the Three, Four, Five States of Matter

Materials are usually made of one of three classes: polymers, metals, and ceramics. Polymers are carbon based molecules that can react to form very complex molecule networks. Metals are the results of combining many metallic atoms together, with all atoms sharing their electrons in a cumulative cloud. Ceramics are the result of the combination of a metal and a non-metallic atom.

States of matter are the properties a certain type of matter has under given pressure and temperature conditions. Consequently, the states are dependent on temperature and pressure, and can never be defined without information on both variables. **Solid matter** has its particles (atoms or molecules) arranged in a spatially defined and shaped structure. Solids can be crystalline (e.g. snowflakes are crystalline ice), or amorphous (e.g. glass is an amorphous ceramic, mostly containing silicon dioxide – sand). They are practically incompressible; their compressibility scale is outside anything observable in the classroom. **Fluids** have a defined volume and are also practically incompressible, but they do not have any defined shape. Their shape is defined by the container they occupy. **Gases** are a loose assortment of particles. The particles within the gases exert almost no attractive forces on each other; have no defined shape or volume.
This is not to say that gases cannot react. In fact, many important chemical reactions occur between gases. For example, the formation of water from hydrogen and oxygen gases. (note: This is not how rain is made.) Particles that make up gases typically travel with speeds of 200 (xenon) to 1200 (helium) m/sec at room temperature and one atmosphere pressure. But since their mass is so small, we do not feel these continuous impacts of the particles on our skin as painful.

In order to create a buzz for a certain topic, some authors use the phrase "4th state of matter." This is, for example, used in articles on corn granaries. Those buildings contain many solid pieces of grain that act, as a whole, like a liquid. This is similar to quicksand. While some of the properties of the complete system are those of liquids, the material itself is still solid. Calling it a 4th state of matter usually simply helps to get a reader's interest, but is imprecise.

Two of the states of matter outside general school curricula are **plasma** and **Bose-Einstein condensates**. Plasma gases are ionized gases as they appear on the surface of the sun, in thunderstorm flashes, or simply in the flame of fires. They are nothing else but gas atoms that have their electron shells temporarily changed and thus glow. Depending on what property you look at, they can be modeled as solid or liquid, but in most cases they still behave like gases. Furthermore, matter can exist as Bose-Einstein condensate, a very cold condensate of matter that only exists under very severe conditions in a laboratory. New states are discovered as we progress in time. This shows that science never stops discovering new things.

Matter Matters:
What's the Matter?

Does Matter Matter?

Oh yes. In fact, matter is really all around us. Even within us. Everything that we touch, see, hear, feel, taste, and smell is matter. What we ARE is matter.

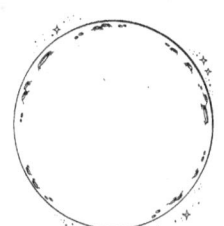

The water you drink? Matter!

The feather you found? Matter!

The stuff you breathe in and out? Matter!

The moon and the sun? Matter!

These are examples of matter. As you might guess, they are all different. We will now learn how they are different, and what that difference means to us. How can we distinguish between them? In order to be able to compare things, we need to classify them first. This is like learning a language when growing up. Only if you speak the language of everyone else can you talk with them. Classification is part of how the "science language" is made. Classification is very simple, and you can do it too!

There are three basic types of matter: gas, liquid, and solid. Gases are, for example, what we breathe. They are part of our atmosphere. They can move around freely and have no defined form. Liquids are, for example, what we drink. Liquids will take the shape of their containers. Solids are hard. They will not change shape if moved into a different container.

Knowing this, can you connect the states of matter to the examples?

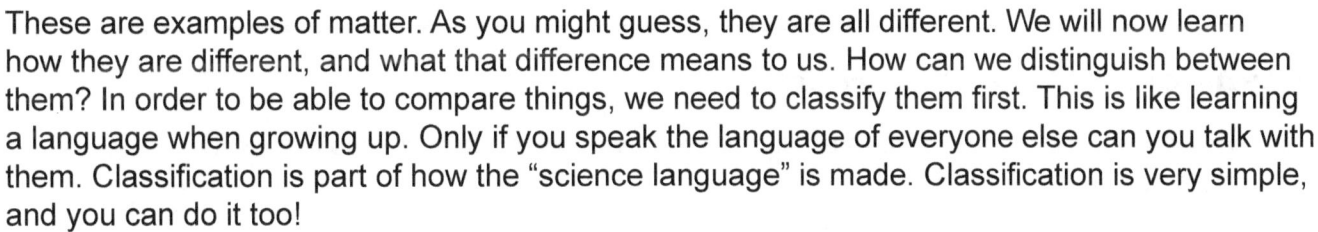

Gas •	• Stone
Liquid •	• Carbon Dioxide
Solid •	• Cola

Now try to apply this "classification" to the matter that surrounds you. Here are some sample questions you can ask yourself:

Is it hard or soft?

What color does it have?

Does it float or sink?

Let's take a look at various materials you have in your classroom and classify them.

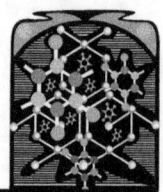

Matter Matters:

Matter Around You

Objective: Learn to classify matter

Equipment: Chalk, earth, water, soap, balloons, and anything else in the classroom can be used. A note on the materials selection: Bring all matter in relation with real-world contexts. Common objects such as desks, coins, pencils, buildings, windows, snowflakes and common substances such as copper, iron, wood, plastic, styrofoam, milk, juice, helium, and water vapor can all be used in this screening experiment.

Procedure: Analyze and categorize the materials around you.

Expansions for the Classroom

The table on the following page can easily be expanded using key curriculum expectations in your state or province, for example:

Texture: Is the surface rough, smooth, waxy, sticky?

Flexibility: Will the material bend on pressure? Is it rigid, stiff, firm, flexible, strong?

Hardness: Using a fork, can you make an impression on the surface? If yes, is it reversible? This can be further expanded with viewing the damages done under a light microscope.

Smell: Does the matter in your hand have any smell at all? Is it pleasant or unpleasant?

Cross-curricular Expansion: If a smell is unpleasant, this is usually an evolutionary biological genetic development to prevent us from ingesting harmful matter. The same is true for taste buds, and the reason why we feel disgust.

States of Matter: solid, liquid, gas.

Expansion for curious students: What matter are flames? (plasma – plasmic gases are ionized gases).

Magnetic Properties: What happens to matter in interaction with a magnet? Does it attract, repel, push, or pull?

Size: Questions can be as simple as: Is it larger/smaller than another object (for a revision of Grades K-5)? What are its dimensions (length, width, height)?

Density: Does it sink or float in water or in oil?

Color: Define color, and relate it to the object.

Matter Matters:
Matter Around You

Shape: What's the matter's shape? Circle, square, triangle, rectangle, oval, etc.

Weight: Is the matter heavy or light? Is it heavier or lighter than another object, e.g. chalk?

Transparency: Does the object let light pass through or block light?

Conductivity: Does the material conduct electricity easily at room temperature? Does the material conduct heat easily?

Material	Is it hard or soft?	Is it light or heavy?	Can you see it?	Does it change its form when you touch it?	What type of matter do you think this is? If you do not know, create your own classification
Balloon					
Your hand					
Water					
Chalk					
Breath					
Find more yourself					

Classify With Class!

Matter is everything that has mass and takes up space. There are three states of matter. Solid, liquid, and gas. All three states contain small particles. Imagine the particles as small spheres. It is what the spheres do with each other that determines the state. In solids, the particles hold on to each other tightly. In liquids, the particles interact loosely. In gases, there is only little interaction between particles. These particles are called atoms or molecules. Molecules are several atoms clumped together. There are many different types of atoms. You might have heard of oxygen or iron.

Take a look at the following table. It summarizes the basic concepts of matter.

Property	Solid	Liquid	Gas
Attractive forces between the particles	Held tightly together by strong attraction	Held loosely together by weak forces of attraction	Have little to no attraction between them
Shape and Volume (in relation to its containment)	Shape and volume defined	Volume defined, shape follows container	Volume and shape free
Compressibility	Cannot be compressed	Cannot be compressed	Compressible
Hardness	Hard	Soft	Immeasurable
Density	High	Medium	Very low

Cool Facts: In the Dark Ages, alchemists used a different classification. They used Earth, Air, Fire, and Water to describe nature. Ultimately, they vainly tried to create gold from thin air. Thus, an alchemist might say that we are 80% Water, 10% Earth, 5% Air, and 5% Fire (depending on our temperament, of course). You can already see this is imprecise. Today, we have a simpler classification system. This shows you how science advances over the years.

Teacher Notes

Introduction of Matter Properties and External Influences:

Students will learn about the effects that external influences such as temperature and pressure have on matter. Consequently, an introduction to the idea of temperature will be given here. Also, students should know that there are different temperature scales, three of which are heavily used, others which have fallen into disuse. Here's a brief overview.

Fahrenheit

A German physicist developed this scale in 1724. The zero point is determined by placing the thermometer in a mixture of ice, water, and ammonium chloride, which cools to a certain temperature that was randomly declared the zero point. Another important point is the level of mercury in the thermometer at average body temperature when held in the mouth or under the armpit. These points are then converted into a scale. This is an arbitrary scale. It is used in the US.

Celsius

A Swedish astronomer by that name developed that scale by arbitrarily appointing the freezing point of water at sea level to be 0 and the boiling point to be 100. Then, he split the system into 100 units. This is also an arbitrary scale with a different step width (1°C > 1°F). It is used in Canada and Europe.

Kelvin

This scale is absolute and scientific, not arbitrary, although it uses the step width of the Celsius scale. The Irish engineer Kelvin discovered that all matter, when cooled, reaches one point beyond which it can no longer be cooled by any method. He set this point as the zero point. This is the scale of utmost importance for science and technology, without which today's society would not be possible.

Rankine

Is a mathematical scale introduced by a Scottish scientist. It is the equivalent scale to Kelvin, but based on the Fahrenheit step width. It is rarely used in practice.

Temperature is a measure of the movement speed of particles that make up matter. The faster these particles move, the hotter the temperature is. Even at room temperature, this movement speed can already be very fast. The gas molecules that make up our atmosphere can travel with several hundred meters per second, and their impingement on our skin is what we feel as warmth; they transfer some of their energy to us by hitting us. Since molecules and atoms are so light, this impact is not felt as pain. (Force = mass * acceleration)

Pressure is a measure of how many particles impinge on a surface at what speeds. The more particles and the higher the speed, the higher the pressure. This shows that temperature and pressure are related. Practically, pressure is the measure of a force applied over a certain area. This is a simple concept: if someone steps on your foot in high heels, the effect is more painful than if the same person steps on your foot barefoot. In this case, while the weight remains constant, the area is larger for the barefoot and the pressure thus less.

It is easy to mix up the concepts of weight and density, a concept that will be taught with experiments later. Density is how much weight a material has within a certain volume.

Let's Get Some Heat!

Temperature Matters – Worksheet

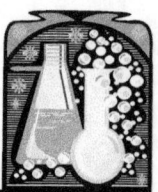

The most important substance for all life that is on this planet is water. Without it, there would not be any life here. In winter, water might freeze outside. In a tea kettle, water boils. The three matter states are dependent on the temperature.

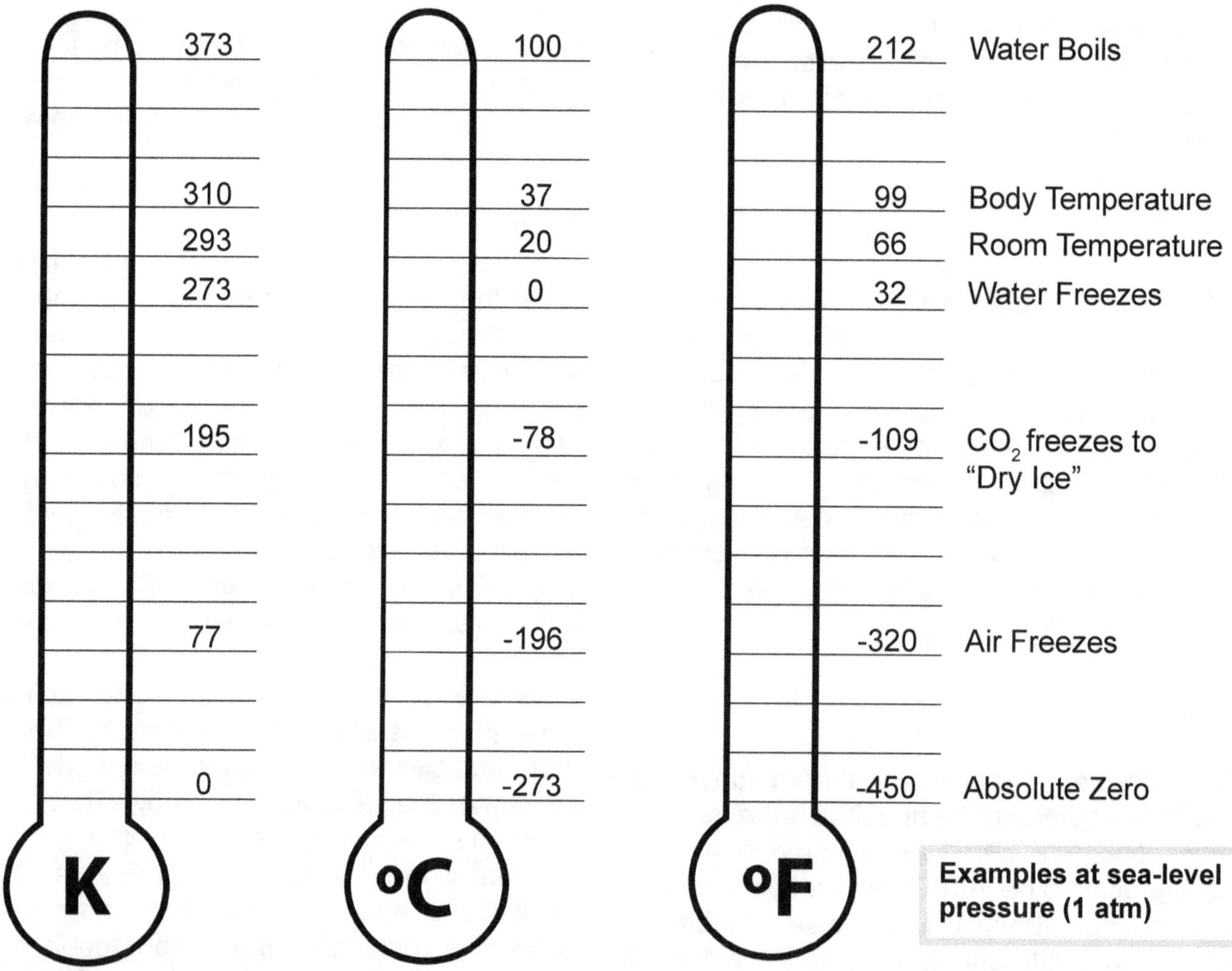

K	°C	°F	
373	100	212	Water Boils
310	37	99	Body Temperature
293	20	66	Room Temperature
273	0	32	Water Freezes
195	-78	-109	CO_2 freezes to "Dry Ice"
77	-196	-320	Air Freezes
0	-273	-450	Absolute Zero

Examples at sea-level pressure (1 atm)

Take a look at the temperature scales above. Answer the questions below.

1) What happens to water at 0°C (32°F)? _____

2) What states is it in at 0°C (32°F)? _____

3) What happens to water at 100°C (212°F)? _____

4) What states is it in at 100°C (212°F)? _____

Hot Calculations

Let's do a cool calculation

1 degree Celsius is not the same as 1 degree Fahrenheit.

So how can you calculate between them?

When will they show the same value at the same temperature?

Here is how you can convert the units:

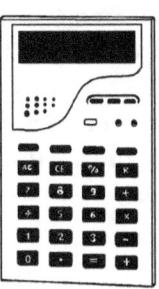

Celsius < - > Kelvin:	[C] = [K] - 273.15	[K] = [C] + 273.15
Fahrenheit < - > Kelvin:	[°F] = ([K] × 9/5) - 459.67	[K] = ([°F] + 459.67) × 5/9
Rankine < - > Kelvin:	[°R] = [K] × 9/5	[K] = [°R] × 5/9

At which temperature do the following scales show the same value?

a) Celsius and Kelvin

b) Celsius and Fahrenheit

c) Celsius and Rankine

d) Fahrenheit and Kelvin

e) Fahrenheit and Rankine

f) Kelvin and Rankine

Why are temperature measurements always taken at sea level?

_____

Find other temperature scales on the World Wide Web and describe them on the lines below.

_____

_____

Cool Facts: In all the above explanations, we assume we are at sea level. That is because we know the pressure there. The higher the pressure, the more particles are present if volume and temperature remain constant. Pressure and temperature influence each other.

- Discuss in the classroom why different temperature scales were invented.

- Why do we measure temperature?

- Which temperature scale is used in which countries?

Pressure, Weather and Equilibrium

Pressure tells us what force particles create on a certain area. Imagine that you dive deep. There is more water above you. The pressure increases. The same is true for the atmosphere. We live at the bottom of an ocean of air. We fly higher. The pressure decreases. Let's make an instrument to measure pressure in class! Air pressure can tell us many useful things. For example, about what weather to expect.

Pressure Experiment

Objectives:
- create a barometer in class and measure air pressure

Equipment:
- base plate 50x15x2cm (wood)
- scale plate 20x15x2cm (wood)
- post 15cm length (wood)
- pivoting pointer 50 cm length, one end sharpened to a point (wood)
- unopened vacuum-packed tin can (e.g. coffee or cashews), ideally with key opener on the lid
- screws/nails
- stiff wire/cable binder or glue/hot glue
- three angle brackets
- screwdriver/hammer, drill

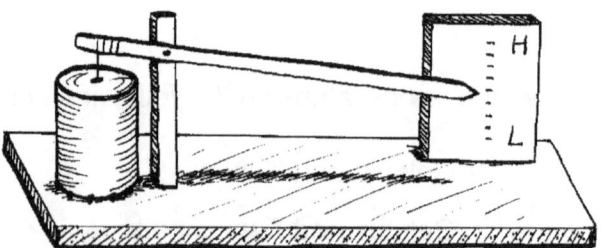

Description:

1. Fasten the tin can securely to one end of the base
2. Fasten a stiff wire or cable binder to the lid of the tin can. You can do that by bending the key opener up. Fix the binder wire there. Hint: prevent snapping off the key by applying a bit of solder. Or glue the binder directly to the tin foil.
3. Fasten the post vertically to the base. Use at least one angle bracket. It must be fixed close to the tin can, towards its center.
4. The pointer is fixed to the post so that its ends can pivot up and down (nail, hole). Connect the pointer's blunt end to the binder wire that was fixed to the center of the can. The other end of the pointer (pointed end) is directed towards the long end of the base.
5. At the long end of the base, connect the scale plate vertically. Use at least two angle brackets. It should be parallel to the pointer and close to it, but not touching.

Explanation: There is a constant amount (mass) of gaseous matter in the can. The inside of the can is in equilibrium with the surrounding atmosphere. Atmospheric pressure can increase due to changing weather conditions. This pressure presses on the lid of the can. The lid is deformed inwards. The matter in the can is compressed. A new pressure equilibrium formed. This is similar to a balance. We add weights to one end. We then have to add the same amount of weight on the other end. We achieve a horizontal, still balance arm in equilibrium. This kind of instrument is used by meteorologists to measure the atmospheric pressure. It is called a barometer.

Expansions (Hygiene, Biology): Most food products are vacuum packed. This avoids deterioration due to oxygen, drying, and insects. Other methods of packaging food for a long life are radiation and drying. High sugar content (jam) and salt content (pickles) are other methods to preserve food.

The Pressure
Worksheet

Create a barometer, either in class or at home.

When the pointer goes up, the pressure in the air increases. When it goes down, the pressure decreases. Note those changes in the following table. Observe changes in weather. Try to find relations.

Date, Time	Pressure Change (up, down)	Weather (rainy/ sunshine)	**Expansion:** Wind direction (get a reading from somewhere in school, or the Internet)

Remember Pressure – for students: Here's how you won't forget the principle of pressure. To help you visualize this concept, imagine this:

You stand on the ground with two feet. You apply a certain force (your weight, which is your mass, times the gravitational acceleration) onto the ground. The pressure the ground feels is the force divided by the area of both your feet. Now stand on the toes of only one foot. Your weight and force remain constant. The area of your contact with the ground changes. You apply the same force over a smaller area. The pressure increases.

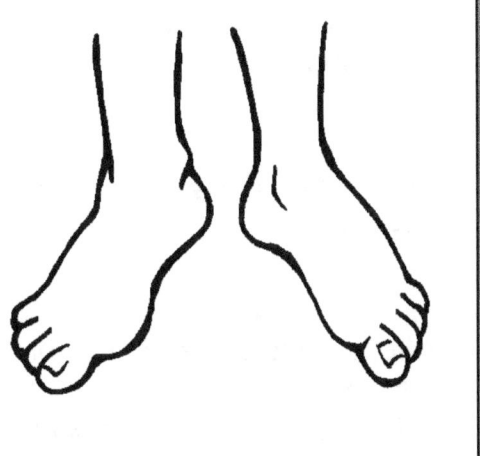

Rise and Shine

Objective: Observe differences in boiling point depending on pressure.

Equipment:

- glass containers that can withstand pressure
- tubes connected to a vacuum system. This can be as simple as connecting a tube with a t-shaped or y-shaped connector to a line with air streaming by
- adjustable heat sock, hot plate or hot water bath
- thermometer

Description:

1. Place liquid inside the shatter proof container and add thermometer.
2. Reduce the pressure inside the container. If possible, measure it.
3. Heat up the water. Control the temperature.
4. Record the temperature at which the liquid boils. Plot that temperature on a graph with the recorded pressure

Explanations: Pressure influences matter. This can be observed if we try to boil potatoes on top of a mountain. The water boils at a temperature below 212°F/100°C. This softens vegetables only very slowly, even after hours of cooking.

Alternative Setup: Fill a large (1 gallon) container with water. Heat the bottom either with a water heating coil or with a hot plate. Measure the temperature on the bottom. Due to the increased pressure at the bottom of the container, the boiling temperature is raised. A thermometer can pick up this increase. The bottom is also closer to the hot plate. This also makes it warmer.

Extension (Physics): The change in melting point of water ice for example, can be calculated. Let's take a quick look at a simple physics equation.

$$p = (v_2 - v_1)T/\lambda$$

Here, p is the actual change of the freezing temperature. This is dependent on the pressure change in degrees/atm. v_2 is the specific volume of the melted substance. v_1 is the volume of the solid in cm³/g. λ is the melting heat in cal/g and T the melting temperature (must be in Kelvin). This is one of those equations that would be impossible without the Kelvin scale.

Rise and Shine

Worksheet

At higher temperatures, the particles move faster. Solids convert to liquids and become gases. Under high pressures, gases become liquid and even solid. This can be seen, for example, in scuba diving gas tanks. The particles are forced closer together. They are less likely to fly apart and change into a gas (boil). Higher pressure means higher boiling point.

Observe the Changes in Boiling Temperature

1. Plot your findings of the experiment here:

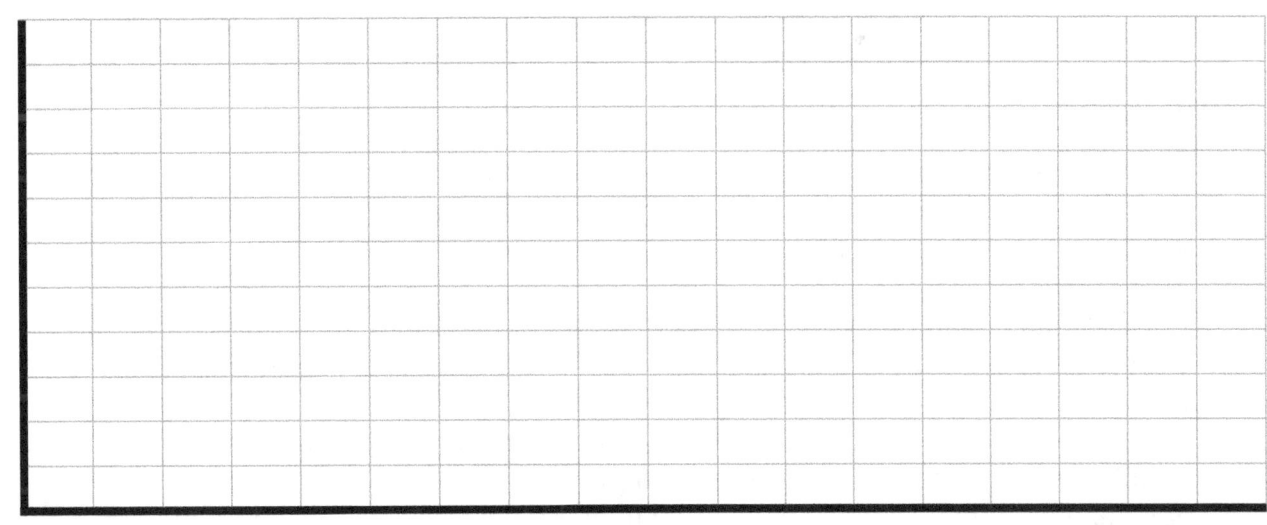

2. How does the Boiling Point Temperature change with pressure? Does the boiling point of a liquid increase with decreased pressure? _____
_____
_____

3. What happened to the Boiling Point Temperature when the pressure was increased? How can you explain that with the Particle Theory? _____
_____
_____

4. Assume you walk to the top of a high mountain. You boil potatoes there in an open pot over a fire. Do you think your potatoes will be ready faster? Or will they take longer? Why?
_____
_____

The Matter Game

- Play out the states of matter in a class setting. Assume each student is a molecule.
- Learn how the change of temperature and pressure typically affects matter.

- All students
- Masking tape
- Open space

Procedure:

1. Tape a large area on the floor in the classroom, hallway or the gym. Area must be large enough for all students to fit and be roughly arms length from one another. Students are to imagine this area as a container. Can also be done with tables as boundaries or no visible boundaries.
2. Let students pretend they are molecules in a solid (for example, ice) within the containment. Let them figure out what to do based on their knowledge of properties of solids. Prod them in the right direction (barely any movement, all bunched together in a defined shape).
3. Tell them the sun is coming out and they are melting. Again, let them figure out what they should be doing based on properties of liquids.
4. Tell them more heat is being added and they are boiling. Let them figure out how they should be behaving as water vapor based on the properties of a gas. Underline that this is not a wrestling match, and that they have to be careful when bumping into each other that they do it gently so no one gets hurt.
5. Remove a piece of tape (or a table) just big enough for one or two 'molecules' to escape.
6. Tell them there is a hole in the container, and see if they find it.

Explanations: Students modeling a solid should gather very close together and vibrate gently. They should not fill or take the shape of their container. The spaces between them should not be large. As a liquid, the spaces between them should be large. They should move in a fluid-like fashion taking the shape of the container, but not filling it entirely. In the gaseous state, they should fill the container, move more quickly, bump into each other and the walls. Students should move in a straight line until they touch the wall or another "student-particle." Gas molecules travel several hundred meters per second. The students should learn this fact after they did this exercise to avoid injury. When the container has a hole in it, the students should randomly, not all at once, move out of the container through the hole. This simulates passive diffusion, not a balloon that ruptured under pressure.

The Matter Game

Worksheet

After observing your fellow students, draw them as they appeared to you.

Solid Classmates	Liquid Classmates	Gaseous Classmates
◯	◯	◯

Discussion:

1. Why were the students/molecules so close together as a solid?
   _____
   _____

2. What is heat?
   _____
   _____

3. What happened when "heat" was added to the classroom? Why?
   _____
   _____

4. Could you convert the gaseous students/molecules back into a solid piece without lowering the temperature? How?
   _____
   _____

5. Research the forces between solids. Which forces exist? Which one is strongest? Why?
   _____
   _____

That's Massive!

Mass, Volume, Density

Every particle has a mass. If mass gets accelerated by gravity, it creates weight. Weight is a force. Mass and weight are not the same! In matter of high density, particles are close together. Solids often have a higher density than liquids. Liquids have a higher density than gases. Density of matter is its mass divided by its volume. A volume is defined as a three dimensional space.

Experiment: Why do ships float?

Objectives:
- Measure volume, mass, and density.
- Determine why ships float.

Equipment:
- container (example: Erlenmeyer or beaker) full of water
- test tubes (glass or plastic)
- nails
- rubber stopper
- graduated cylinder (small and large)
- balance

Description:

1. Measure the volume of the test tubes. Measure the diameter **d**. Measure the height **h**. Then calculate $(d/2)^2 \times \pi \times h$. This is the volume of the tube. Write it down. (π is the circular constant relating the circumference of a circle to its diameter with a value of 3.141).

   The volume of the tube is _____ cm³.

   A second method to measure volume is this: Close the tube with the rubber stopper. Fill the large graduated cylinder with water. Mark down the height of the water. Submerge the closed tube. Do not hold your fingers under water. Mark the new line. Deduct the first number from the second. Write down the volume in the space above. Did you get the same volume for both measurements? _____ (yes/no)

2. Measure the weight of one nail, the tube and the stopper. Use a balance. Write it down.

   The weight of one nail is _____ g.

   The weight of one stopper is _____ g.

   The weight of one tube is _____ g.

That's Massive!

Mass, Volume, Density

3. Close the tube with a stopper. Put it into the container with water, rubber stopper first. Does it float? If yes, add two nails. Repeat the procedure until it starts sinking. Add your data into the following table. The total weight is the weight of all nails, plus the stopper, and glass weight. Calculate the density by dividing the total weight by the volume.

Number of Nails	Total Weight	Volume	Density	Floats/Sinks

4. Look at the table after you sunk the "boat". What was the density of the boat when it sank? The density of the boat (tube) when it sank was _____ g/cm³.

5. Did the volume change when the mass changed? ___ yes ____ no

6. Measure the density of water. Weigh a small (50ml) graduated cylinder. Fill it with 50ml water. Subtract the first value from the second.

   The mass of 50ml water is _____ g.
   The volume of 50ml water is _____ cm³ (1ml=1cm³).
   The density of water is _____ g/cm³.

7. We observe that objects with a lower density _____ (float/sink) in a liquid of higher density.

8. Can you explain why ships float? _____

___

Cool Facts:

We breathe air and are slighter less dense than water. Divers need metal belts to increase their density to dive down. Also: If you can't remember how to calculate density, check this out. **Density is Mass over Volume.** In short: This looks like a heart, cut in half!

Oily Icing

We all know that ice floats on water. But why? It's a solid. We learned that solids have a higher density than liquids. Water is anomalous. It reaches its highest density at around 39°F (4°C). Ice has a lower density than liquid water. It floats. Does oil float on water? Oil and water do not mix. The molecules are immiscible (see section on mixtures). Let's see what happens if we combine ice, oil, and water.

Objective:
- Learn about density and density changes upon phase changes.

Equipment:
- transparent container
- vegetable oil
- water
- ice cubes with frozen-in food color

Procedure:

1. Fill your cup to ¾ height, half with water, half with oil.
2. Let the liquids settle for a minute.
3. Add a colored ice cube. Observe its melting behavior.

Explanation Quiz Based on Your Observations:

1. Compared to oil, the density of water is…

    a. higher   b. lower   c. the same

2. Compared to oil, the density of ice is…

    a. higher   b. lower   c. the same

3. Upon melting, the density of water…

    a. increases   b. decreases.   c. doesn't change   d. all three

4. If the density of water is highest around 39°F (4°C), water will expand when it is heated above 39°F (4°C).

    a. correct   b. incorrect

Just Hot Gas!

External Influence of Temperature on Gaseous Matter

Objective: ♦ Determine how different temperatures influence gases.

Equipment:
- boiling water
- ice cold water and ice cubes
- thermometer, for a more scientific approach
- empty small plastic water bottle without a top or an Erlenmeyer flask
- rubber balloon
- container large enough to hold the plastic water bottle (Erlenmeyer or bowl)
- tweezers or tongs

Procedure:

1. Blow up a balloon in order to stretch it. This reduces stiffness within the rubber. Let the air out.
2. Identify what state of matter is within the empty bottle or Erlenmeyer.
3. Place the balloon over the top of the plastic bottle or Erlenmeyer.
4. Place the balloon-bottle or balloon-Erlenmeyer combination in a bowl of water. The water has just been boiled. If you use glass, make sure it is heat resistant. Otherwise, it might burst from thermal shock in the boiling water. Hold glass in boiling water. Hold for several minutes. Use tweezers or tongs.

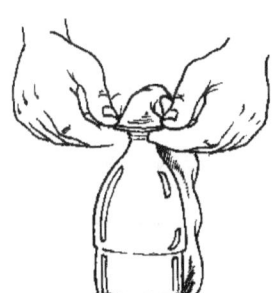

5. Record your observations on the worksheet.
6. Using the particle theory of matter, explain your observations on the worksheet.
7. Remove the balloon-bottle combination from the hot water. Immediately place it in ice cold water. Wait until it is cooled.
8. Record your observations on the worksheet.
9. Using the particle theory of matter, explain your observations.

Explanations: The balloon inflates (not completely, and very slowly) in hot water and deflates in cold water. This can be related to the particle theory of matter. Molecules speed up with a rise in temperature. They move out of the container fast enough to inflate the balloon. The gas molecules move more slowly when cooled. There is no additional air created due to the temperature increase. The gas expands. There is more empty space between gas particles. The same mass of gas occupies a larger volume. The density decreases. This is why hot air balloons can fly.

Flashy extension (Physics): This effect can be brilliantly displayed by dropping inflated balloons into liquid nitrogen. The balloon volume reversibly shrinks to almost nothing.

Just Hot Gas!
Worksheet

Draw the balloon as it appears during the experiment.

Balloon just attached	Balloon with heated air	Balloon with cooled air

Discussion:

1. Why did we blow up the balloon to stretch it first?
   _____
   _____

2. Why does the balloon expand when the bottle is immersed in hot water?
   _____
   _____

3. What happens with the particles inside the bottle with the balloon when it's heated?
   _____
   _____

4. Do we increase the amount of gas inside the balloon while heating?
   _____
   _____

5. Why does the balloon contract when the bottle is immersed in cold water?
   _____
   _____

6. What happens with the particles inside the bottle with the balloon when it's cooled?
   _____
   _____

Just Hot Gas!

External Influence of Temperature on Gaseous Matter

Objective:
- Determine how different temperatures influence gases.

Equipment:
- boiling water
- ice cold water and ice cubes
- thermometer, for a more scientific approach
- empty small plastic water bottle without a top or an Erlenmeyer flask
- rubber balloon
- container large enough to hold the plastic water bottle (Erlenmeyer or bowl)
- tweezers or tongs

Procedure:

1. Blow up a balloon in order to stretch it. This reduces stiffness within the rubber. Let the air out.
2. Identify what state of matter is within the empty bottle or Erlenmeyer.
3. Place the balloon over the top of the plastic bottle or Erlenmeyer.
4. Place the balloon-bottle or balloon-Erlenmeyer combination in a bowl of water. The water has just been boiled. If you use glass, make sure it is heat resistant. Otherwise, it might burst from thermal shock in the boiling water. Hold glass in boiling water. Hold for several minutes. Use tweezers or tongs.
5. Record your observations on the worksheet.
6. Using the particle theory of matter, explain your observations on the worksheet.
7. Remove the balloon-bottle combination from the hot water. Immediately place it in ice cold water. Wait until it is cooled.
8. Record your observations on the worksheet.
9. Using the particle theory of matter, explain your observations.

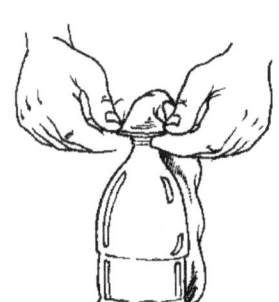

Explanations: The balloon inflates (not completely, and very slowly) in hot water and deflates in cold water. This can be related to the particle theory of matter. Molecules speed up with a rise in temperature. They move out of the container fast enough to inflate the balloon. The gas molecules move more slowly when cooled. There is no additional air created due to the temperature increase. The gas expands. There is more empty space between gas particles. The same mass of gas occupies a larger volume. The density decreases. This is why hot air balloons can fly.

Flashy extension (Physics): This effect can be brilliantly displayed by dropping inflated balloons into liquid nitrogen. The balloon volume reversibly shrinks to almost nothing.

Just Hot Gas!
Worksheet

Draw the balloon as it appears during the experiment.

Balloon just attached	Balloon with heated air	Balloon with cooled air

Discussion:

1. Why did we blow up the balloon to stretch it first?
   _____
   _____

2. Why does the balloon expand when the bottle is immersed in hot water?
   _____
   _____

3. What happens with the particles inside the bottle with the balloon when it's heated?
   _____
   _____

4. Do we increase the amount of gas inside the balloon while heating?
   _____
   _____

5. Why does the balloon contract when the bottle is immersed in cold water?
   _____
   _____

6. What happens with the particles inside the bottle with the balloon when it's cooled?
   _____
   _____

Press it!

External Influence of Pressure on Density

Objectives: ♦ Determine the compressibility of a material.

Equipment:
♦ stones
♦ water
♦ syringe
♦ balloons

Procedure:

1. Identify the state of the three materials in the table and enter your observations.

2. Try to compress each material.

3. Take a stone and press it. Observe changes in the stone.

4. Fill a syringe with water. Hold the open end with a finger and try compressing the syringe. Does it move?

5. Remove the water from the syringe and try to compress the gas inside with one finger on the end. Try to compress the balloon.

Materials	State	Compressible/Not Compressible
Stone		
Water		
Gas		

Cool Facts:

1. If you compress a gas inside your syringe, it will get warm. Compressing gases increases temperature. Try it with a bicycle pump. Hold one end closed. Compress the pump. Feel the pump getting warm. Reducing gas density makes them colder. This is how your fridge gets cold.

2. Foams are mixtures of gases and liquids or gases and solids. Put a snowball (mix of sugar, cream, and gas) inside a low pressure container. It will vastly increase its size. The same will happen inside a microwave. The gases inside the snowball expand when heated. This can become messy.

The Swirl of Hot Color!

Influence of Temperature on Solid and Liquid Matter

Objectives:
- Learn about the influence of temperature on particle speed.
- Observe diffusion in a material.

Equipment:
- boiling water
- hot tap water
- cold tap water
- ice cold water
- thermometer, for a more scientific approach
- clear plastic or glass cups/containers, for example Erlenmeyers
- food coloring
- ice cubes
- heat source (sun, hairdryer, electric radiator)

Procedure:

1. Fill four clear plastic cups or glasses with water (half full). Each glass should be filled with water of a different temperature. Add ice cubes to the coldest glass.
2. Record the temperature of each glass with a thermometer.
3. Add four drops of food coloring to each cup. Do not stir. Make sure the drops land on the ice in the coldest cup.
4. Record observations on the worksheet.
5. Using the particle theory of matter, explain your observations.

Explanations: The food coloring moves more quickly in the hot water. This can be explained with the particle theory of matter. Increasing the temperature will increase particle speed. The water molecules move more quickly in the hot water. The food coloring moves more quickly. The food coloring does not go inside the ice cubes. Movement of liquids (color) within solids (ice) is very slow. This is called diffusion.

Extensions (Chemistry): Coat a simple chemical like $KMnO_4$ (potassium permanganate) in icing sugar and drop it into a liquid like water. This will prevent the solute from dissolving too early, while it still sinks to the bottom. This usually creates convection currents, and the principle of passive diffusion might be confused by the students if an uncoated $KMnO_4$ pellet is used. By coating the chemical in a material that dissolves without a color effect, diffusion can be shown. Speed or diffusion depending on temperature (heating the water) or concentration (more $KMnO_4$) gradients can be shown.

The Swirl of Hot Color!
Worksheet

Make a drawing of how the color looked in the COLD water when it was...

... just entered	... after 1 minute	... after 5 minutes

Make a drawing of how the color looked in the HOT water when it was...

... just entered	... after 1 minute	... after 5 minutes

Discussion:

1. At which temperature did the color diffuse faster through the water? Hot or cold? Why?
   _____

2. What do you think would happen if the water was actively boiled?
   _____

3. Did the color mix within the ice cubes? Why or why not?
   _____

Some Honey, Honey?

Viscosity experiments

Objectives:
- Define what "viscosity" is.
- Determine the viscosity of matter.

Suction Experiment #1

Equipment:
- straws
- glasses or cups
- ice cream
- water

Marble Drop Experiment #2

Equipment:
- marbles
- transparent graduated cylinders
- water
- honey (transparent, liquid)
- sunflower oil
- stop watch

Shear Experiment #3

Equipment:
- 2 rectangular mats, letter sized (can be hard plastic, or sponge rubber)
- water
- honey
- vegetable oil
- weight (has to be the same weight in the same position each time)
- force meter (typically a spring with a scale)

Some Honey, Honey?

Viscosity experiments

Procedure:

Suction Experiment

1. Fill a cup with water, and another glass with frozen ice cream fresh from the freezer.
2. Stick a straw into each glass and suck.
3. Observe what happens, and draw your conclusions with regards to viscosity from it.

Marble Drop Experiment

1. Fill one graduated cylinder with water, one with vegetable oil, and one with honey, all to the same level.
2. Carefully lower a marble to the surface, and release it.
3. Measure the time it takes for the marble to sink to the bottom, or past each graduation on the cylinder
4. Observe what happens, and draw your conclusions with regards to viscosity from it.

Shear Experiment

1. Place one of the polymer sheets on a table.
2. Spread the liquid you want to investigate on the sheet.
3. Place the second sheet on top, then place the weight on top.
4. Attach a force meter to the upper sheet (example: by punching a hole into the sheet with a hole puncher).
5. Pull the sheet slowly, until it moves. Continue pulling it with this constant force. Record the force necessary.
6. Observe what happens, and draw your conclusions with regards to viscosity from it.

Cool Facts: Look at viscosity as how "un-liquid" a liquid is. The easier it flows, the more liquid it appears, and the less viscous it is. The higher the viscosity of matter, the more interactive forces act between its molecules.

Also Amazing: Glass is an under-cooled liquid, NOT a solid. However, the viscosity is so high that we effectively do not observe it with the eye. Old lead glass tends to move over the decades, which is why old glass windows distort the light when we look through them. Gases and solids also have viscosities. Those can be measured in scientific labs.

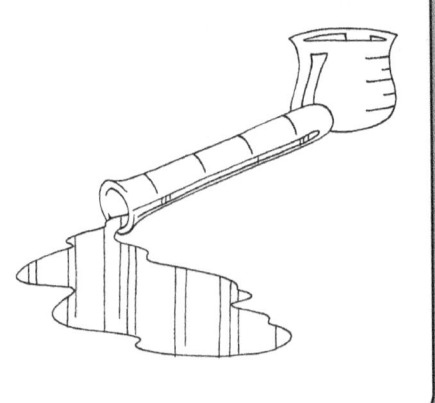

Some Honey, Honey?

Viscosity Experiments Worksheet 1

Observations with the suction experiment: Look at the surface of the water in your cup from the side. Compare it to the surface of the ice cream. Draw the difference:

Water Surface	Ice Cream Surface

1. Suck the liquid through the straw. Describe how it feels and what happens to the straw:

   a) Water: _____

   b) Ice: _____

2. Based on this observation, which liquid do you think is more viscous? Remember that viscosity describes how un-liquid matter is.

   _____ is more viscous, because the straw _____.

Observations with the Marble Drop Experiment:

3. Draw where the marble was after 1 second.

Water	Vegetable Oil	Honey

Some Honey, Honey?

Viscosity Experiments Worksheet 2

4. Now write down the time it took for the marble to sink to the bottom. Measure the height. Determine the speed of the marble. Divide height by time.

	Water	Vegetable Oil	Honey
Time (sec.)			
Height			
Speed (cm/sec.)			

5. When matter is viscous, it makes it more difficult for other matter to pass through. So, look at your experiment results. Which liquid do you think is more viscous?

   _____ is more viscous, because the marble _____.

Observations with the Shear Experiment:

6. The more viscous matter is, the more difficult it is to shear it. How difficult was it to pull the sheets? Write down the force it took to move the sheet.

	Water	Vegetable Oil	Honey
Force (N)			

7. Based on your findings, which liquid do you think is more viscous?

   _____ is more viscous, because the force it took to shear two sheets was

   _____ (highest or lowest?).

Teacher Notes

Matter Changes in the Classroom: PHYSICAL CHANGES

Phase changes can happen between all states of matter. We are most used to phase changes in water. That is mainly due to the fact that there is plenty of water on this planet. We can also easily create the temperatures under which the phase changes in water occur under atmospheric conditions. When water freezes, it forms ice crystals that we can observe in winter at many places. When heating water, it is transformed into a gas: water vapor. We can only see this water vapor since it condenses into tiny liquid droplets in cool air. In clouds, this process occurs due to adsorption of water molecules on the surface of impurities in the air. Fog can also be created in the classroom. A simple method to do so is to use a bicycle pump to increase the pressure inside a small wetted plastic bottle closed with a rubber stopper. Once the stopper pops out, fog can be observed inside the bottle. Upon a sudden drop in air pressure, liquid particles quickly transfer into the gas phase. There are consequently an excess of liquid particles dissolved in the air. They precipitate out as shortly visible droplets indicating that a new equilibrium has been reached. Other experiments that observe the effect of impurities in the air are described in this chapter.

Water is one of the few exceptions in nature: When water freezes, its density is reduced. That is why ice swims on water. The opposite usually happens with most other materials where the frozen solid state has a higher density than the liquid state. The particles become more ordered and more tightly packed when changing from a gaseous to a liquid to a solid state. Even below the freezing point of water, liquid water molecules can enter the gas phase. This change of state is called sublimation. We cannot observe the actual phase change with our eyes, but some of its effects are shown in this section. That is why uncovered food in the freezer "burns." It slowly dries out. This sublimation can easily be observed in frozen carbon dioxide (dry ice).

Under atmospheric pressure, carbon dioxide does not exhibit a liquid phase. Heated dry ice will emit carbon dioxide gas, but not melt. The evaporating carbon dioxide cools the surrounding air. Water from naturally occurring air humidity condenses. Cold air can dissolve less water molecules than warm air. It forms fog. The fog visible around cold objects like dry ice is only water. The emitted carbon dioxide remains invisible to us. The reason for the fog to form is the cold temperature of the dry ice, not the carbon dioxide gas.

Phase changes in matter occur due to an input of energy. This energy overcomes the chemical bond energies of materials, first melting and then evaporating them. Since different materials have differently strong bonds, the transition temperatures differ. A further significant input of energy can overcome the attractive forces between an atomic core and its electron. The resulting state, plasma, glows. This is a side effect of electrons falling back into place around the stripped atoms. This can be seen, for example, in a candle flame.

Matter resulting from incomplete burning of a candle in a flame is black soot, which is mainly amorphous carbon. Solids can appear amorphous (disordered), for example, glass. Some solids can also crystallize. Physical changes (mainly ordering the atoms due to crystallization) of carbon can produce diamond, as well as carbon soccer balls (Buckminster fullerenes) and nanotubes. Other atomic configurations of matter created by physical changes are discovered all the time.

Students will learn to name the phase changes (evaporation and condensation, liquefaction and solidification, and sublimation and re-sublimation), and relate them to examples. They will also learn to assign reasons to the changes, such as pressure or temperature changes.

Let's Get Changed!

Exchanges Between States

How do states of matter change? Simply put, if you heat a material, it will change its state. This will usually happen from solid to liquid to gas. Sometimes, solids change into a gas, and are never liquid. Carbon dioxide is such a material under atmospheric conditions. Take a look at the following graphic. It shows the concept of heating up a material and its phase changes.

Each addition of energy creates a change in state

SOLIDS +E LIQUIDS +E GASES +E PLASMAS

Here you can see what the changes between states are called.

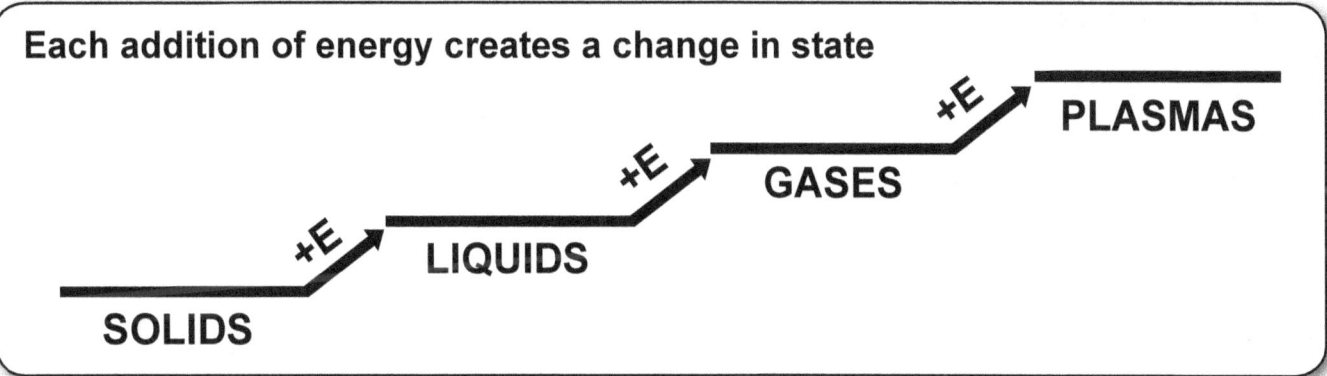

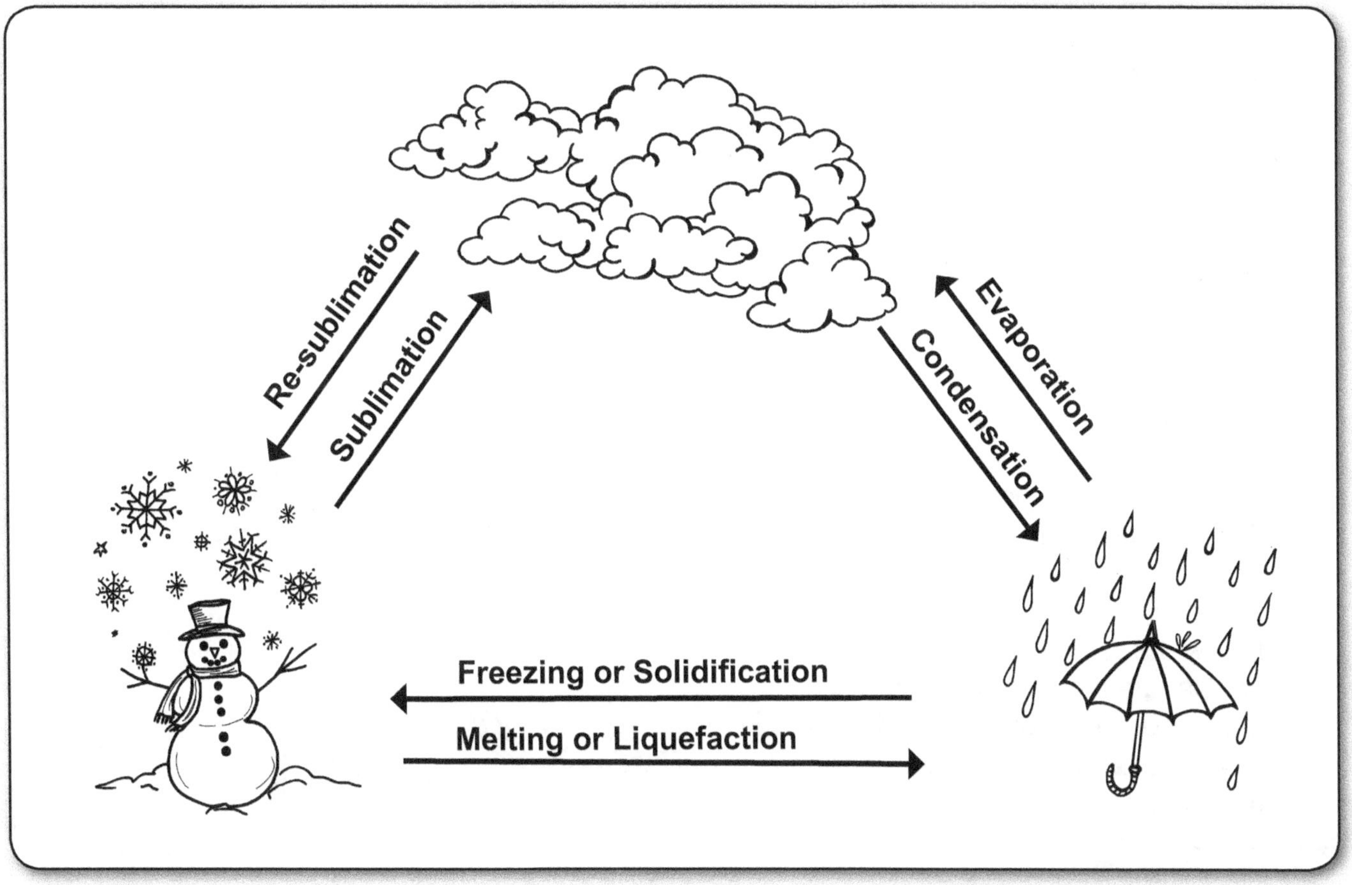

Re-sublimation / Sublimation

Evaporation / Condensation

Freezing or Solidification

Melting or Liquefaction

Let's Get Changed!

Exchanges Between States Worksheet

Extension (Informatics – Library/Data Gathering): Do some research at home online:

The following examples are all transitions between states. Find out at what temperature and pressure they might happen. The first one has been done for you. You can use any Internet search or encyclopedia to help you.

1. **Solid → Liquid:** Water ice melting <u>Water, T=273.15K, p=1 atm</u>

2. **Solid → Liquid:** Melting of dry cleaning solvent (CCl_4) _____

3. **Solid → Gaseous:** Carbon dioxide (CO_2) sublimation _____

4. **Liquid → Solid:** CO_2 solidification from liquid

5. **Liquid → Gaseous:** Iron evaporation _____

6. **Gaseous → Solid:** Graphite deposition from gas phase _____

7. **Gaseous → Liquid:** Nitrogen liquefaction _____

Cool Facts: An old German tradition at New Year's Eve is to melt pieces of lead and tin on a spoon, then pour them quickly into a bucket of water. The resulting shapes were used to tell the fortune of the next year. It is a fun tradition that allows everyone to melt some metal and observe liquid metal with their own hands. Lead melts already at 600.6K (621.4°F, 327.4°C), far below the temperature of a candle flame. Candle flames burn with temperatures between 600°C (1112°F) and 1400°C (2552°F) in different parts of the flame.

Creating Clouds 1

The formation of clouds in the skies can be simulated in the classroom.

Objective:
- Create cloud condensation in the classroom

Equipment:
- isopropanol (a.k.a. iso-propyl alcohol, C_3H_8O)
- water
- thick-walled Erlenmeyer flask or bottle
- rubber or cork stopper (fitting the flask) with hole
- short glass or hard plastic tube (10 cm each), fitting the stopper hole
- polymer hose (>30 cm) snugly fitting the glass tube and pump
- air pump (for example, a bicycle pump)

Procedure:

1. Mix isopropanol and water in a ratio 1:1 (for example 100 ml of each)
2. Pulverize some chalk and sprinkle it into the mix.
3. Push the glass tube through the stopper. Fix the hose to its end. Fix stopper to the bottle neck.
4. Connect the other end of the hose to an air pump and make sure it is airtight on both ends.
5. Increase the pressure in the bottle by pumping in air.
6. Once the pressure is high enough, it will pop out the stopper, and clouds will appear.

Explanation: Upon a sudden drop in pressure (for example, the popping of the stopper), liquids with a high vapor pressure will evaporate. The air is oversaturated with water leading to condensation. Chalk dust provides condensation nuclei on which water droplets form: fog.

Creating Clouds 2

The formation of clouds in the skies can be simulated in the classroom. Dirt in the air can facilitate the creation of clouds. This experiment shows that particles we create in the air help to form clouds.

Objectives:
- Create cloud condensation in the classroom.
- Relate condensation to dirt particles in the air.

Equipment:
- water
- thick-walled Erlenmeyer flask (the larger, the more clouds can be seen)
- rubber or cork stopper (fitting the flask) with hole
- 1 short glass or hard plastic tube (ca. 10 cm) fitting the stopper hole
- Polymer hose (>30 cm) snugly fitting the glass piece
- box of matches
- gas pump (or use your lungs)

Procedure:

1. Wash the inside of the jug thoroughly
2. Pour water into the jug to a height of approximately 3 cm.
3. Push the glass tube through the stopper. Fix the hose to its end. Fix stopper to the bottle neck.
4. Shake the closed container thoroughly. This will saturate the air inside with water vapor.
5. Increase the pressure. Blow air into the jug from your lungs. Keep the elevated pressure by pinching the hose.
6. Make sure the stopper does not fly into you if you blow in too much air.
7. Release the pressure suddenly.
8. Observe if there is any cloud formation.
9. De-pressurize the flask with your lungs. Suck out air this time. To hold the lowered pressure, pinch the hose again.
10. Light a match.
11. Hold the match close to the end of the hose. Blow it out. Simultaneously open the tube.
12. Observe how the smoke is sucked into the flask.
13. Repeat steps 5 through 7 with soot particles inside the bottle.
14. Observe the cloud formation.

Creating Clouds 2

Explanation: When releasing the pressure initially, no or few clouds are visible. After introducing soot, clouds are observed more easily. We find that soot particles help in the formation of clouds. Clouds form when pressure or temperature drops occur. Water vapor that is always present in the air condenses. This water vapor is measured by meteorologists as air humidity. Condensation is visible as clouds. They consist of many small water droplets. They scatter light. That is why we see them. Without nuclei, the differences in pressure that we create in the flask are too small. The cloud formation remains invisible to our eye. It is too short and too faint.

Extensions (Physics):

- Pressure and temperature could be measured in the jug.
- Place the flask on an overhead projector for an increased visual impact. Reduce the lighting in the room. The cloud might appear to "glow." It scatters the light of the projector. If the bottle is heated too much by the projector, visible condensation might no longer occur.
- Use a gas lighter instead of a match. No effect is observed since no soot particles are produced.

Creating Clouds 1 and 2 Worksheet

Fill in the following sentences. Choose the correct one of the given possibilities.

1. Clouds are formed when pressure _____.
   (increases, decreases, remains constant)

2. Clouds on our planet are an assembly of many _____ droplets.
   (air, methane, water)

3. Rapidly reducing pressure forces _____ water molecules out of the water.
   (more, less, the same)

4. However, we cannot see them since they are in the form of _____.
   (droplets, single water molecules)

5. When we light a match in front of an opening with lower pressure, we _____ soot particles.
   (suck in, blow out)

6. These particles _____ water droplet formation. They are called nuclei.
   (help with, prevent)

7: We _____ see water droplet.
   (can, cannot)

The Cloud Game

Play out the formation of clouds in a class setting. Assume each student is a molecule. Learn how the change of pressure and presence of soot particles affects water condensation.

Equipment:
- all students, some with colored head bands, hats or caps
- masking tape
- open space

Procedure:

1. Tape a large area on the floor in the classroom, hallway or the gym. The area must be large enough for all students to fit and be roughly arms length from one another. Students are to imagine this area as a container. This activity can also be done with tables as boundaries, or no visible boundaries. Direct students accordingly.

2. Let students pretend they are liquid water molecules within the container. Let them figure out what to do based on their knowledge of properties of liquids. They should be loosely together at the "bottom" of the container. Only one or two students are evaporated. They slowly fly "above" the liquid.

3. Tell them the container is being pressurized. Any free flying molecules should go back to the bulk water.

4. Inform them that the pressure is released suddenly. All the students facing the "hole" in the container should start to drift into the air. They do not touch each other. Tell them that they are so small, they cannot be seen by the eye as single molecules.

5. Insert soot particles (several more students wearing distinctive headbands or caps, depending on space availabilies).

6. Tell them that the container is being pressurized once more. Any free flying molecules should go back to the bulk water.

7. Inform them that the pressure is released suddenly. All the students facing the "hole" in the container should start to drift into the air. This time, they agglomerate on the soot particles, at least three per soot particle. Tell them that now they become larger water droplets that are visible as clouds.

Explanations: Students modeling a liquid should move in a fluid-like fashion taking the shape of the container, but only filling the bottom. All liquids have a vapor pressure, meaning that there are molecules floating above the bulk liquid. This is also true for solids, but much less pronounced. Upon releasing the pressure quickly, more liquid molecules escape into the gas phase. They condense on the container walls or on dust in the atmosphere. They are so small that they are usually not visible. With the introduction of water droplet nuclei such as soot, the escaping water molecules condense in mid-air. The forming water droplets become large enough to scatter the light. We can then observe this phenomenon.

The Cloud Game

Worksheet

Gaseous molecules escape from solid and liquid matter all the time. This is called vapor pressure. Most fall back and become solid/liquid again. The more molecules escape, the higher the vapor pressure. The higher the atmospheric pressure, the fewer molecules can escape. We increase the pressure. The gaseous water molecules are forced back into the water. After a sudden release of total pressure, many water molecules escape the liquid. They become gaseous water. They condensate quickly. In clean air, we cannot see them. In dirty air, evaporated water molecules will condensate on the dirt particles. They form droplets which we can see. This is fog or clouds. Our air always contains some small particles. Around streets, the air contains much more particles emitted by cars. Most of them are dangerous for us.

Observe your fellow students and yourselves. Draw them as they appeared to you. Use blue for water molecules and red for soot particles.

Pressurized Liquid	Liquid molecules after a quick pressure release	Pressurized Liquid with soot particles in the atmosphere above it	Clouds forming on the particles after sudden pressure loss

Discussion:

1. We pressurize the container. Why do we have less gaseous water molecules?

2. The pressure is reduced suddenly. What happens to water molecules?

3. What effect do the soot particles have?

Cool Facts: If we could increase the pressure a lot, the water would freeze. Even at or above room temperature. This can happen in specialized high pressure laboratories.

Extensions: Health Sciences - Small particles are inhaled. They can enter our blood stream and cause strokes and heart attacks. They can also stay in the lungs and cause cancer. Find out more about damaging dirt particles from cars and motorcycles online.

Slightly Sublime

Objectives:
- Observe the drying of wet clothes while frozen.
- Relate the findings to everyday science. Freezer burns, for example.

Equipment:
- towel or piece of cloth
- balance
- freezer or rack outside at a temperature constantly below 0°C (32°F)

Procedure:

1. Thoroughly wet a piece of cloth with water. Wring it so it does not drip.

2. Deposit the cloth in a freezer. If possible, hang it outside. Make sure that the temperature outside will never heat up to 0°C (32°F) for at least one week.

3. Weigh the frozen cloth regularly (once every 2-5 days). Weigh quickly because it must not thaw and lose liquid water. If you live in a cold area, weigh it outside.

4. Make a graph of the weight change over time in the worksheet.

Explanations: Water constantly sublimates. It becomes water vapor, without ever becoming a liquid, even below the freezing point of water. This happens much slower than water evaporating. This method can be used to dry clothes outside slowly. Even in the middle of winter, this does not work in regions that are rainy or too warm – use the freezer instead. Put the cloth on a rack with thin struts inside the freezer. Otherwise it will freeze solidly onto the walls. This can be done as a home experiment.

Extension: The same can be observed in frozen foods. If the packaging is not airtight, water will evaporate. This is called freeze burn. While freeze burn meat looks rotten, it is not. No bacteria typically grow on properly frozen food. The taste is off though. Even ice cubes slowly vanish inside the freezer.

Slightly Sublime

Worksheet

1. You can dry your clothes outside in the middle of a freezing winter. Take a look at all the different changes between states. What do you think happens?
   _____
   _____
   _____

   You can do this as an experiment at home or in the class.
   Take a cloth, for example a towel. Make it thoroughly wet. Wring it out so it does not drip anymore. Put it in the freezer on a grille. After it is solidly frozen, measure its weight once a day. Record the weight in the graph below. Make sure the cloth never thaws while you weigh it. Best do the weighing outside if the temperature is below freezing point.

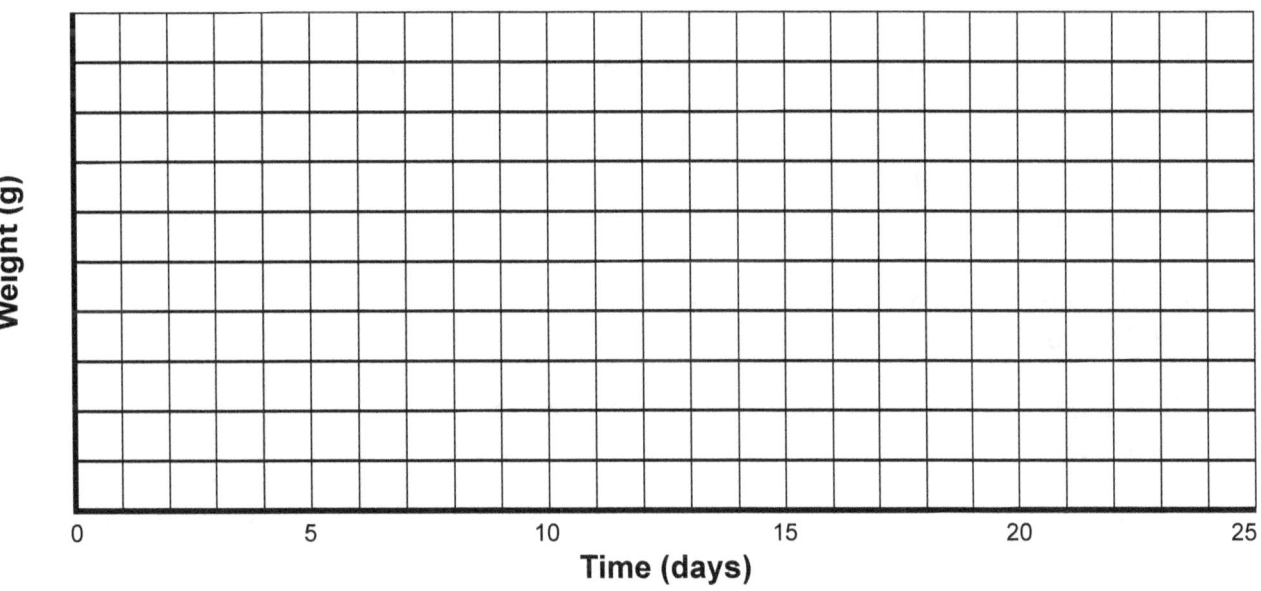

2. What do you observe?
   _____

3. Why do you think this is happening?
   _____

4. What other experiment could you do to back your hypothesis?
   _____

5. Now that you know about sublimation, explain freezer burns. Would this food make you sick?
   _____

CO_2 Fun

Objectives:
- Create a temperature curve baseline while heating water.
- Establish that water only boils at 100ºC (212ºF) under atmospheric pressure.
- Establish that bubbling in water does not mean it is at 100ºC (212ºF).
- Record the temperature of dry ice in water.

Equipment:
- dry ice
- water
- ice cubes
- thermometer
- heater (can be Bunsen burner or hotplate)
- laboratory glassware (for example beaker, or Erlenmeyer)

Procedure:

1. Place a few ice cubes in cold water in a transparent container. Stir and measure temperature.
2. Start heating at a constant, low setting.
3. Record the temperature every 30 seconds while stirring all the time.
4. Mark the time and temperature when a) all ice is melted and b) steam is observed for the first time.
5. Once the mixture boils, stop the experiment.
6. Create a graph using the template in the worksheet. Plot temperature over time, starting at zero.
7. Take another cold water beaker. Stir and measure temperature.
8. Enter dry ice cubes, stir and measure temperature. Record your observations. Is the water still?
9. Blow carefully on the surface. Record the observations. Relate them to the hot water experiment. What similarities do you see? Why do you think these phenomena occur?
10. Repeat steps 7-9, but use hot water (circa 50°C, 122°F) instead.

Explanations: This experiment shows melting point and boiling point. Close to these points, temperature changes become very slow. If you heat ice water, it will remain at 0°C (32°F) as long as there is ice left. This becomes very obvious when the results are graphed. It is beneficial to stir the liquid regularly to evenly distribute heat. Water evaporation starts at zero degrees and becomes visible above 50° (122°F). We can see the steam because the air above the boiling water is cool. The water condenses.

CO_2 Fun
Worksheet

Plot the temperature of the heated water over time on the following graph

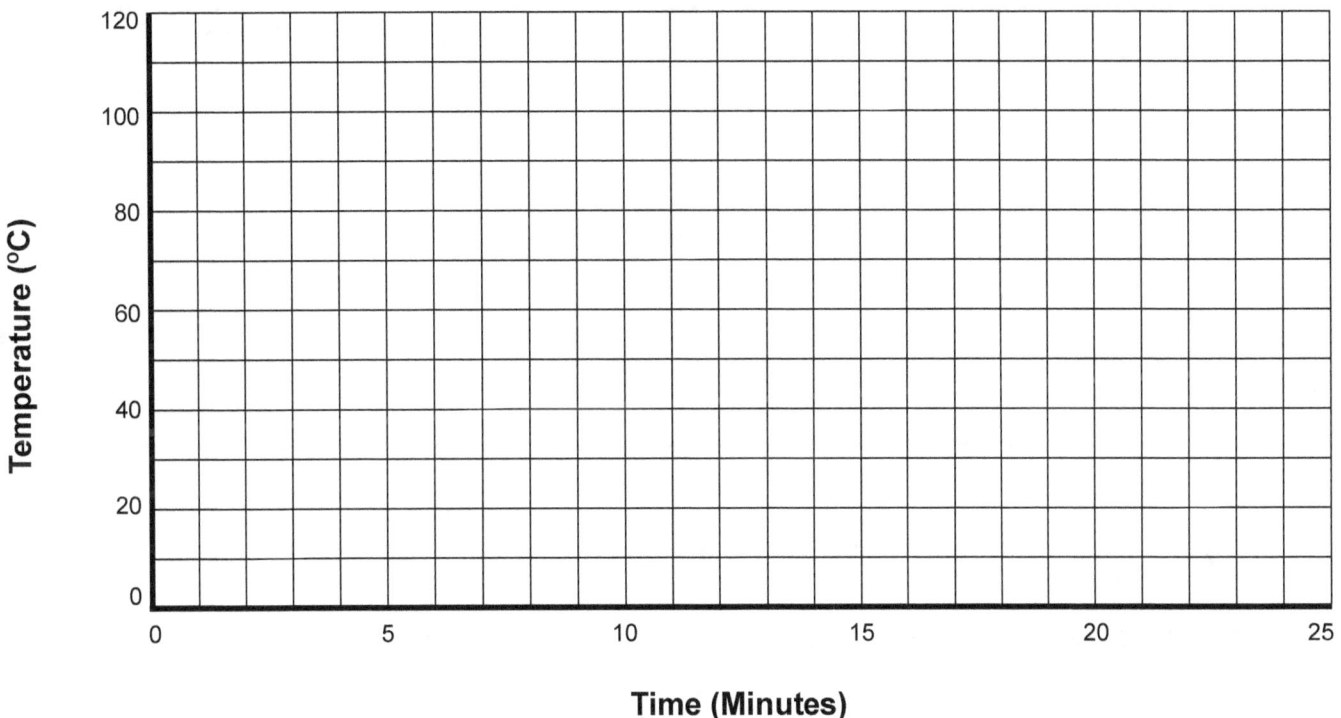

Based on this graph, answer the following questions with true or false.

T F 1. We slowly heat the water and ice cubes mixture. The temperature in the water increases.

T F 2. We slowly heat the water and ice cubes mixture. The temperature inside the ice cubes increases.

T F 3. We slowly heat the water and ice cubes mixture. The temperature inside the ice cubes decreases.

T F 4. We slowly heat the water and ice cubes mixture. All ice cubes are melted. The temperature in the water increases quickly.

T F 5. The rate of temperature increase is the same throughout the whole experiment.

T F 6. We slowly heat the hot water and steam mixture. The temperature in the water increases.

T F 7. We slowly heat the hot water and steam mixture. The temperature in the steam increases.

Cool Facts: Extremely hot water steam can ignite paper, since it can reach temperatures above the flash point (350°C, 662°F) and even the ignition temperature of paper (450°C, 842°F).

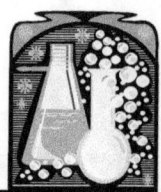

CO_2 Fun

Worksheet

Draw the difference of dry ice behavior in warm water at 122°F (50°C) and in cold water at 34°F (1°C).

Dry ice in warm water	Dry ice in cold water

8. Why is the difference between CO_2 in warm and cold water observed? Explain.

9. What happens to the water surrounding the dry ice? Which temperature does it approach?

10. Is the water boiling when the dry ice is entered? Which gas forms the bubbles?

11. What happens if ice forms on the surface of the dry ice? Is it permanent?

12. There is cold white vapor forming above the dry ice. There is also hot white vapor forming above boiling water (at 212°F/100°C)? Note down the differences. Which one rises?

13. The cold vapor sinks to the floor. Why?

14. What happens to a flame caught in the cold vapor? Why? Is it the vapor that does this?

15. Soap bubbles blown into a container with dry ice start hovering. Why?

Cool Facts: Repeat the experiment, but add a pH indicator like red cabbage juice, thymol blue or phenolphthalein into the water. It will display a color change. This is indicating that CO_2 makes water acidic. We can do the same with our breath? We exhale some CO_2. If we blow into water through a straw, we make it more acidic.

CO_2 Fun
Worksheet

Plot the temperature of the heated water over time on the following graph

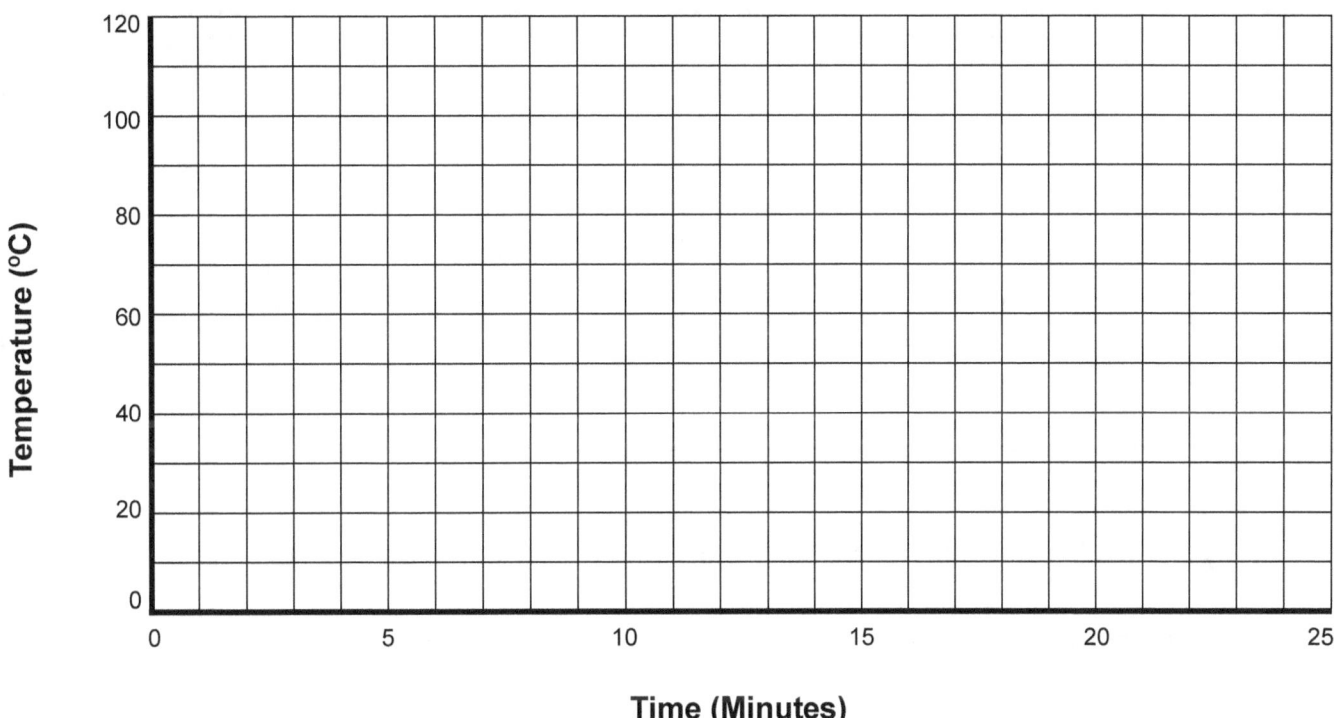

Based on this graph, answer the following questions with true or false.

T F 1. We slowly heat the water and ice cubes mixture. The temperature in the water increases.

T F 2. We slowly heat the water and ice cubes mixture. The temperature inside the ice cubes increases.

T F 3. We slowly heat the water and ice cubes mixture. The temperature inside the ice cubes decreases.

T F 4. We slowly heat the water and ice cubes mixture. All ice cubes are melted. The temperature in the water increases quickly.

T F 5. The rate of temperature increase is the same throughout the whole experiment.

T F 6. We slowly heat the hot water and steam mixture. The temperature in the water increases.

T F 7. We slowly heat the hot water and steam mixture. The temperature in the steam increases.

Cool Facts: Extremely hot water steam can ignite paper, since it can reach temperatures above the flash point (350°C, 662°F) and even the ignition temperature of paper (450°C, 842°F).

CO_2 Fun
Worksheet

Draw the difference of dry ice behavior in warm water at 122°F (50°C) and in cold water at 34°F (1°C).

Dry ice in warm water	Dry ice in cold water

8. Why is the difference between CO_2 in warm and cold water observed? Explain.
   _____

9. What happens to the water surrounding the dry ice? Which temperature does it approach?
   _____

10. Is the water boiling when the dry ice is entered? Which gas forms the bubbles?
    _____

11. What happens if ice forms on the surface of the dry ice? Is it permanent?
    _____

12. There is cold white vapor forming above the dry ice. There is also hot white vapor forming above boiling water (at 212°F/100°C)? Note down the differences. Which one rises?
    _____

13. The cold vapor sinks to the floor. Why?
    _____

14. What happens to a flame caught in the cold vapor? Why? Is it the vapor that does this?
    _____

15. Soap bubbles blown into a container with dry ice start hovering. Why?
    _____

Cool Facts: Repeat the experiment, but add a pH indicator like red cabbage juice, thymol blue or phenolphthalein into the water. It will display a color change. This is indicating that CO_2 makes water acidic. We can do the same with our breath? We exhale some CO_2. If we blow into water through a straw, we make it more acidic.

CO_2 Fun

Extension

Objectives:
- Observe different densities of gases
- Observe different properties of gases
- Relate observations to real life applications

Equipment:
- candle or glow stick
- detergent/water mixture (~1:10) or soap bubble solution
- soap bubble maker (e.g. straws, rings, pipe cleaners)
- styrofoam box or large beaker (min. 2L)

Procedure:

1. Deposit dry ice into an empty Styrofoam box. Wait until vapor comes out the top.
2. Light a candle or glow stick. Carefully pour the vapor over the flame. Take notes.
3. Put the box back on the floor. Wait until no more air currents are visible in the vapor.
4. Blow soap bubbles into the Styrofoam container. Observe what happens to the bubble. If a transparent container is used, everyone can see what is happening inside.

Explanation: CO_2, carbon dioxide, is heavier than air. It sinks to the ground. People used to take a candle with them into mines or cellars. If the candle extinguished, there was no oxygen left, and it was important to return quickly. Carbon dioxide replaces the oxygen on the floor. The candle light goes out. Some fire extinguishers work that way. Blowing soap bubbles into the frozen CO_2 container shows this, too. The bubbles sink in air, falling into the container. Soap is heavier than air. At some point, they will start hovering. At this point the density of air in the bubble, plus soap, is the same as the CO_2 surrounding it.

Crystal, Crystal on the Wall

The Alcohol of Thyme

Objective:
- This experiment is a demonstration experiment aimed at showing crystallization from a melt.

Equipment:
- overhead projector
- tongs or heat protection gloves
- Petri dish
- thymol (enough to cover the whole bottom of the Petri dish)
- heater (can be hot plate, tea light, tea warmer, or other device capable of heating above 140°F [60°C])

Procedure:

1. Melt the thymol sample. It melts above 126°F (52°C).
2. Place the dish on the overhead projector. Wear proper heat protection.
3. Let cool slightly. If unperturbed by vibration, the liquid will super-cool. This means it is colder than its melting point, yet still liquid.
4. Add small crystals (e.g. thymol) to your super cooled thymol liquid. They will act as crystallization points.

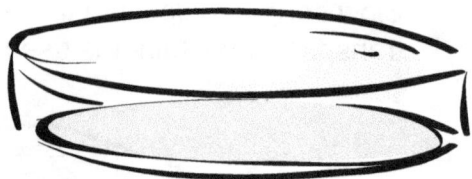

Explanations: The cold solid thymol crystals will start the crystallization. As the crystals spread through the melt, they produce interesting shadow patterns. These can be magnified and projected on the wall.

Cool Facts: Thymol is an organic molecule. It is found in the oil of thyme. It has antiseptic properties. That is why it is often used in mouthwashes.

Extensions: Geology: Igneous Rocks and Crystal Formation.
Crystals of all sorts can be found in every rock. All were formed from a melt. The core of our planet is all liquid. Very interesting patterns and colorations are observed in bismuth crystals, which are commercially available.

Crystal, Crystal on the Wall

Extensions: Engineering

Materials Engineering Departments at universities usually have samples of crystallization trees of iron, from hand-sized to human sized, which can often be borrowed upon kind request.

Extensions: Other Materials

This experiment can be performed with a large variety of materials other than thymol. Some have to be performed inside a fume hood. Supersaturated sodium thiosulfate or sodium acetate solutions can be seeded with crystals to nucleate crystallization. Also, simple cooling in air of molten naphthalene (moth balls) or salol will result in interesting crystallization patterns. Crystal lacquer is an easy material to use. A thin layer of lacquer is spread on a microscope slide. While the solvent evaporates, crystals form, nicely visible on an overhead projection. Methylene blue, urea, or enalapril are other materials that produce beautiful crystallization patterns. The effect can be observed in even more detail. Use microscopes with polarization filters. Super-saturated solutions of sugar, salt or borax in water also slowly crystalize upon evaporation. This will be expanded upon in the next sections.

Using the boxes below, draw how the crystal formation looked. Describe how they were growing.

Drawing:	Notes:

Teacher Notes

Matter changes in the classroom: CHEMICAL CHANGES

Matter can not only undergo physical changes due to external influences such as temperature and pressure. But there is also the possibility of changing matter through chemical reactions. These reactions transform the type of matter. Chemical bonds between the atoms are broken and formed.

The section also deals with the fact that each reaction has an environmental impact. The science that deals with how matter runs through a useful life for human use is called life cycle analysis. More and more states and provinces in North America have started to incorporate the ideas from life cycle analysis into their curricula throughout many different topics. A very good interactive online movie, that can easily be projected in a classroom setting, on this topic was produced by Dr. Leonard and is freely available online as *"The Story of Stuff."*

One of the major chemical reactions that constantly changes matter all around us is oxidation. Every metal will invariably oxidize, although some do so more easily than others. Gold and platinum are notoriously difficult to oxidize, while aluminum and silicon form native oxides the moment they are exposed to the least bit of oxygen. Oxygen atoms form a new material together with the metal. The most evident is rust, the result of combining iron and oxygen. This oxide layer on iron is non-protective, as opposed to Al and Si oxides, which are very protective. Our aluminum foil always stays shiny: it forms a thin layer of dense aluminum oxide (Al_2O_3, a.k.a. sapphire). Rust is structurally inferior to metal. It is no longer a ductile metal, but has transformed into a brittle ceramic. Corrosion and oxidation damage cost in the United States surmounts to an incredible $276,000,000,000 annually – that is 3% of the Gross Domestic Product (GDP). And when bridges collapse as a result of corrosion, many lives can be in danger.

In this section, the effects of various environmental conditions on simple metallic objects such as nails will be shown. Students will explore why some materials prevent oxidation and corrosion and others do not.

Another type of chemical change of matter is explored in this section. This is the chemical transformation of solids and liquids into gases. Familiar chemical changes of this type include the mixing of cement or baking with sodium bicarbonate (baking soda). In both cases, CO_2 is produced. It makes the cake rise. CO_2 is also used in fire extinguishers. It works by replacing the oxygen necessary to sustain a fire. Another chemical reaction explored is the reaction of H_2O_2. Oxygen gas is produced with the help of a catalyst. A catalyst speeds up a reaction that would otherwise take a long time to proceed.

A great change in matter that is very effective in a classroom setting, but requires a fume hood, is the carburization of sugar. There are several ways of doing this, two of which are presented here. By adding an acid to the sugar, the sugar is dehydrated. The water leaves the sugar, and is emitted as steam since the reaction produces heat. After all, sugar is a very good fuel, one that we use to move around ourselves. The reaction can also be done without acid, by igniting a mixture of sugar and lighter fluid. The black snake that is generated is pure carbon and is hot for some time. This experiment can nicely lead into a discussion of crystal structures, commencing with carbon and its allotropes (see page 42).

Making a Fire Extinguisher

Most people have fire extinguishers in their homes. They are often required by law. Many fire extinguishers work by replacing oxygen. Oxygen is a gas. It is one of the critical ingredients for a fire. Without oxygen, there can be no fire. A fire is a very quick oxidation. In this experiment, you can make a fire extinguisher yourself!

Equipment:
- large bowl
- small dish
- baking soda
- short candle (e.g. tea light) and a long candle in stand
- match or lighter
- vinegar

Procedure:

1. Fill the small dish with baking soda.
2. Place both candles upright in the baking soda.
3. Place the dish on the bottom of the large bowl.
4. Light both candles.
5. Pour the vinegar into the dish of baking soda. Take care not to flood the candles.
6. Observe which candle extinguishes first.

Explanation: Vinegar and baking soda react and produce carbon dioxide gas. The carbon dioxide gas is heavier than air. It sinks into the bottom of the container. As the reaction continues, more and more carbon dioxide gas is produced. It slowly fills up the bowl from the bottom upwards. When the carbon dioxide has risen to the level of the flame, the flame will go out. It has no more oxygen to burn. That is why the short candle goes out first.

Chemical Creation of Gases and Heat

Objectives:
- Observe how chemical reactions can create heat and gases.
- Inflate a balloon with a simple chemical reaction.

Equipment:
- large (250 or 500 ml) Erlenmeyer flask
- hydrogen peroxide (H_2O_2, >30% conc.) – do not let students handle this
- metal oxide powder (Manganese oxides (MnO or MnO_2) and rust (Fe_3O_4) work well). Most oxide powders will do.
- balloon
- spoon

Procedure:

1. Fill about 25 ml of hydrogen peroxide (30% conc.) into the flask.
2. Take a spoon full of metal oxide and fill it into the balloon.
3. Attach the balloon to the mouth of the flask. The powder should not fall in. The balloon containing the metal oxide will hang limply from the opening of the glass container.
4. Hold the balloon upright. The powder will fall inside and react with the H_2O_2. This reaction creates oxygen gas.
5. Observe the speed with which the balloon inflates.
6. For an experimental series, use three different amounts of hydrogen peroxide. For example 10, 25, and 50 ml. Observe differences in the speed and volume of the balloon inflation. Touch the bottom of the flask with care. It gets warm during the reaction.

Explanations: In nature, things often decompose and change at a slow rate. If you leave water in a cup on your porch, it will eventually evaporate. This could take a long time. Hydrogen peroxide contains oxygen and hydrogen. There are two atoms of each element per hydrogen peroxide molecule. Oxygen is part of air that we breathe. 21% of air is made of oxygen. Over time the oxygen is released as a gas from the H_2O_2 liquid. Hydrogen peroxide then becomes water and oxygen. This reaction is very slow and we do not notice it. We can use catalysts to speed up reactions. The metal oxide powder brings the reaction to occur within seconds rather than weeks. The hydrogen peroxide breaks down into water and oxygen. The oxygen will inflate the balloon slightly. The catalyst remains unchanged. White water vapor can be seen because of the heat produced. It comes hissing out of the mixture. The oxygen gas is invisible to human eyes.

Extension: After the reaction is completely over, the balloon can be removed. A glow stick can be stuck into the open Erlenmeyer. The rate of oxidation will increase. The glow stick will be brighter. This shows that the gas created, oxygen, is promoting flames. This should be done inside a closed fume hood. Make sure to wear appropriate safety gear.

Chemical Creation of Gases and Heat

Worksheet

Describe the experiment in two sentences.

Use the following terms: Hydrogen peroxide, catalyst, oxygen, water, inflation, metal oxide

_____
_____
_____
_____

Discussion:

1. Hydrogen peroxide can be used to generate a gas. Which gas is that? How could you find out?
   _____

2. Where else have you maybe seen hydrogen peroxide before? Maybe in a hair salon. What is its purpose there?
   _____

3. Suggest a chemical reaction.
   _____

4. What do you think the metal oxide powder is used for?
   _____

5. Did the metal oxide powder change somehow? If yes, why? If no, why not?
   _____

6. Will the balloon inflate more with more metal oxide catalyst powder? _____

7. Will the balloon inflate more with more water in the bottle? _____

8. Will the balloon inflate more with more H_2O_2 in the bottle? _____

Extension: H_2O_2 and MnO_2 also make a cool rocket. Take a film canister, put H_2O_2 into the canister and the metal oxide into the lid. Close it and watch it pop! The canister and lid can be decorated with fins and caps. This can also be done with water and alka seltzer or vinegar/lemon juice and baking soda.

React-it Other Chemical Reactions:

Metal Degradation

Many of the reactions we observe are oxidations. The opposite is reduction. Oxidation means we steal some of the electrons from an element. You can imagine that it is like taking away planets from a star. Iron oxidizes to brown iron oxide or rust. Materials can also corrode in contact with liquids. This can transform a useful material into something less useful. This does not require oxygen from the air. We all oxidize carbon all the time. We eat carbon containing molecules (that's what food essentially is). Then we breathe in oxygen. Our body oxidizes the carbon. We breathe out carbon dioxide, a gas.

Objectives:
- Observe chemical changes in matter.
- Record your observations.

Equipment:
- 9 nails (use iron or mild steel, not stainless steel)
- 9 transparent beakers (height about the same as the nails)
- grease (any grease will do, Vaseline, butter, etc.)
- distilled or de-ionized water
- paint (not water soluble, oil paint works well)
- salt (NaCl), ca. 50g
- clinging foil

Procedure:

Fill six of the beakers half full with water. Add 50g of salt to three of these water beakers. Leave the remaining 3 beakers dry. Label each series of three beakers "salt water," "water," and "dry." Now, prepare the nails. Cover three of the nails in grease. Cover three more in paint and let them dry. The other nails leave bare. Enter one nail of each kind into one beaker of each kind. There should, for example, be one bare nail in a dry beaker, one in a water beaker, one in a salt water beaker, and so forth. For reproducibility studies, you may prepare and use more than one nail of each type. Only use one nail per beaker for randomization. This avoids the nails influencing each other. Prevent water from evaporating by covering up the top of the beaker with the foil. Record your observations once every day at the same time for one week. Some water may evaporate. Fill each beaker up to its initial level each day. Use distilled water. This reduces influences of matter found in water.

Discussion: Distilled or de-ionized water does not contain many impurities. Some of these impurities are called ions. Ions transport electric charges. Ions in the water speed up corrosion. In the oceans, salt ions transport the charges around. The more ions, the faster this happens. That is why iron transforms into rust faster in contact with sea water. This is dangerous for metallic ships. The hull must be protected, for example with paint. Often, this paint is not environmentally friendly.

React-it Other Chemical Reactions:
Metal Degradation Worksheet

Use the table below and draw, in color, how your nail looks. In your drawing, you can draw the differently prepared samples into the same beaker, even if they were in separate containers in your experiment. Also, enter the water line in each case.

Dry	Water	Saltwater	Day (or Week)
			0
			1
			2
			3
			4

Black Sugar Snake 1

Some matter changes (reactions) are reversible. You can run them one way. And you can run them backwards. Many physical reactions are reversible. You can thaw and re-freeze ice as often as you want. That is, until the water has sublimated and evaporated as water vapor and you have no solid or liquid left. The state of the matter changes. The particles remain the same. Many chemical reactions are irreversible. Matter is transformed into another type of matter. The reaction cannot go backwards. One of these reactions is the black sugar snake.

Snake 1: The Snake From Acid

Equipment:
- sugar
- water
- sulfuric acid, concentrated (treat with care, use proper gloves, safety glasses and must experiment in fume hood)
- beaker
- safety equipment (safety glasses, lab coat, etc.)
- fume hood

Procedure:

1. Wet the sugar with a small amount of water in the beaker.

2. Stir in some concentrated sulfuric acid. The reaction produces lots of heat, steam, and sulfur oxide fumes. The reaction smells like a mixture of rotten egg (sulfur) and fresh caramel.

3. The white sugar turns into black carbon. It bubbles and grows out of the beaker.

Explanation: We dehydrate (remove water from) sugar with sulfuric acid. Sugar is a carbohydrate. When removing water, all that remains is carbon. Carbon is usually black. We do a similar thing when making caramel from sugar. We chemically change (here we "polymerize") the sugar. If we heat it too much, it burns. The burnt stuff is mostly carbon.

Black Sugar Snake 2

Snake 2: The Burning Snake

Equipment:
- sand
- alcohol or lighter fluid (this is the fuel for the snake)
- baking soda
- icing sugar
- spoon (any size)

Procedure:

1. Mix 4 spoons of powdered sugar with 1 spoon baking soda.
2. Make a mound with the sand. Push a depression into the middle of the sand.
3. Pour the fuel into the sand to wet it.
4. Pour the sugar and soda mixture into the depression. Pour some lighter fluid on top.
5. Ignite the mound, using a lighter or match. Must be done inside a fume hood or outdoors.

Explanation: At first, you'll get a flame and some small scattered blackened balls. Then, the CO_2 gas will puff up the carbon. A continuous snake will form. Sodium bicarbonate breaks down into sodium carbonate, water vapor, and carbon dioxide. Oxidizing the sugar produces water vapor and carbon dioxide gas. The snake is carbonate blackened by carbon particles.

Cool Facts: Diamond is also just carbon, but arranged in an orderly fashion. The carbon atoms had a physical change. They transformed from graphite into diamond. Diamond and graphite oxidize (burn) to carbon dioxide gas at several hundred degrees. We exhale that same gas. Our body organizes the chemical change from carbon in food to carbon dioxide gas. Indoor fireworks often contain unhealthy heavy metals such as mercury. Stick to these snakes instead! Go outside when lighting up indoor fireworks.

Black Sugar Snake 1 & 2

Worksheet

Notes: Use this space to draw how the matter (sugar) looked before and after the experiment.

Drawing (before):

Notes: The black snake smelled like _____
Caramel is burnt sugar. Sulfur is within the acid.
Other notes:_____
_____
_____
_____
_____

Drawing (after):

Matter Waste

Environmental Impacts of Reactions

Everything we do creates an impact on our environment. There is no single reaction that does not influence the world around us. Everything we eat has to be grown. Everything we wear will eventually be thrown away. Every time we drive, we produce harmful emissions. All our trash ends up on smelly landfills. Many chemicals create problems for animals in the oceans. Pollutants in the air cause diseases in humans and animals, and can change the earth's climate.

Objectives:

- Observe the effect of pollutant on our environment.
- Play the Game of Life.

Equipment:

- 1 large bucket
- 1 object per student (e.g. stones)

Procedure:

1. Arrange yourselves in a row.

2. Imagine that each of you holds an item you bought, or the emissions from a travel you made.

3. Start with an empty bucket on one side. Add each of your items.

4. Explain to your classmates what it is. Also, explain how this pollutes. For example, fertilizers wash into rivers. Diesel particles create dangerous matter to breathe. To produce 1 kg of meat, 7 kg of wheat have to be pumped into an animal, etc.

5. Give a suggestion how you think this impact could be reduced. For example, use less fertilizer, use diesel particle traps, and eat vegetarian. The bucket will become heavier along the line. This weight is similar to the impact that all of us have on the environment. The more humans there are on the planet the greater the impact.

Teacher Notes:
Mixtures and Solutions

In nature, we often find matter not as a single substance, but in mixtures. A simple mixture is the one we walk through and breathe in every day: Air. Air is a mix of varying amounts of over a dozen different gases. The main component of air is nitrogen. Approximately 78% of our air is nitrogen, N_2. This is very advantageous for us since it is an inert gas. It does not generally react at room temperature, is non-flammable, and non-toxic. Slightly less than 21% of our atmosphere is oxygen, O_2. This gas allows us to walk around outside water, and still oxidize carbon (food) in our cells. It is also, together with hydrogen, one of the components of water, H_2O. The third most abundant gas in our atmosphere is Argon, making up less than 1% of the volume of the air. It is a single-atomic gas. The main reaction product of organic oxidation is carbon dioxide gas. The level of CO_2 is currently at about 0.033%. During the times of the dinosaurs, the level was much higher, and scientists calculated that the weather was tropical all around the globe, with no icecaps.

Other simple mixtures are sea water. A multitude of salts, like the table salt sodium chloride, NaCl, dissolve in water. This is a mixture of a solid and a liquid. In this case, the solid dissolves in the liquid. This just means that the atoms of the solid can fit in between the liquid molecules. The solid does not vanish, we just cannot see it anymore. The sand at the bottom of the sea creates mud. This is a mixture of a solid and a liquid where the solid does not dissolve in the water. We can also mix liquids, for example, water and alcohol. Some liquids do not mix. The two liquids are "immiscible." Oil and water is such an example. Solid mixtures are, for example, steels or amalgams. They combine different atoms (mainly metals) into a uniform product that we call an alloy. Other examples of solid mixtures are rocks and sand. Rocks are also crystallized liquid. The center of our earth is hot enough to melt even stones. Due to the motion of tectonic plates, some stones get pressed towards the center of the earth, while other material emerges elsewhere. Most of the matter from this melted mixture hardens (crystallizes), forming solid mixtures. Rocks as well as metals often contain many different types of matter frozen in place together. Sands are ground stones. A simple method to separate rocks by shape and size is to sieve them. Other methods such as sedimentation make use of material density.

In this section, students will learn to determine whether materials in every day life are single phase materials, or whether they are mixtures. They will be able to explain what mixtures are, and determine the contents of materials. The mixtures analyzed include milk, sew water, smoke, fog, pop, tar sand, paper, clay, and gold. The students will distinguish between different colloidal states of mixture (microscopically separated components) and solutions (atomically mixed) mixtures. They will classify substances found at home as pure substances, solutions or mechanical mixtures.

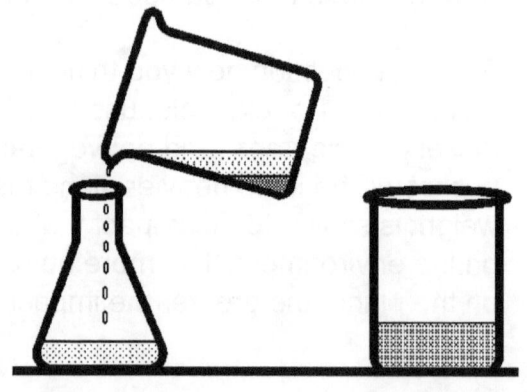

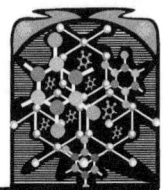

Mix it, Shake it, Separate it

An Introduction to Miscibility

Mixtures of matter are all around us. We can mix gases in gases. Air is a mixture of more than a dozen different gases. We breathe all that mixture in every day. The main gas in the atmosphere is called nitrogen. When we mix liquids and gases, we can have fog (water in air) or a fizzy pop drink (carbon dioxide gas in sugary water). A combination of gas and solids is smoke (air and dust). Clay and mud are mixtures of liquids and solids. The following table contains some examples of mixtures.

Mix ⇩ into ⇨	Gas	Liquid	Solid
Gas	Air	Pop, soap bubbles	Hydrogen storage in metal hydrides
Liquid	Fog	Alcohol in water, oil in water (e.g. mayonnaise)	Water in a sponge, ground water, tar sand
Solid	Smoke	Clay, salt water	Steel (mix of different metals)

Cool Facts: Gold is never really pure gold. Those juicy gold nuggets might look like gold. They probably are also mainly gold. But they always contain trace amounts of silver, copper, and/or platinum. This is a mixture of one solid in another. It contains several elements. A mixture like this is called an "alloy." Metals are seldom pure. Most metals contain other elements. All these mixtures are alloys. Engineers and scientists produce special alloys. Stainless steel, for example, is iron or nickel alloyed with other elements. It improves the usefulness of steel by making it oxidation resistant. Other alloys become harder or more flexible due to this kind of matter mixing.

In fact, selecting the wrong alloy often results in disaster. In the first half of the last century, many welded ships broke apart in cold waters. The chosen steel alloy became brittle and broke like glass. The most notable were the US Liberty class ships. Some of them even broke in harbor.

Mix it, Shake it Separate it
Worksheet

Objectives:

♦ Determine the phase and mixture of materials you know.

Equipment:

♦ Different solids and liquids you find in your kitchen or the classroom.

Procedure:

Take a look at the list exercise below, and fill in the blanks. Find material properties from the internet for samples not available to you. Add more materials that you find in your classroom. One example is given for you. Most of the following mixtures are colloids.

1. Milk is a <u>liquid/liquid</u> mixture of <u>water</u> and <u>oil</u>. The small droplets of oil make the water appear white.

2. Smoke is a _____ mixture of _____ and _____. The soot particles darken the air.

3. Clouds are a _____ mixture of _____ and _____. UV light is not stopped by clouds, we can still get sunburn even with a cloudy sky.

4. Pepsi (or Coca Cola) is a _____ mixture of _____ and _____. It is a fizzy drink. The water has been further treated with sugar, sweeteners, artificial flavors, colors and acid. This is the only solution in all these examples.

5. Blood is a _____ mixture of _____ and _____. The solid cells that make our blood appear red contain iron. When iron oxidizes, it gets dark brown. So does blood in air. It is the same reaction.

6. Tar sands are a _____ mixture of _____ and _____. Separating the oil from the sand requires vast amounts of energy, and produces a heavy environmental footprint.

7. Find your own examples: _____ is/are a _____ mixture of _____ and _____.

© On The Mark Press • S&S Learning Materials ◀ 70 ▶ OTM-2137 • SSB1-137 The Nature of Matter

 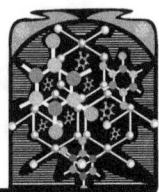

Solu-what?

An Introduction of Solute, Solubility, and Concentration

So what's all this "solubility?" Some particles can dissolve other particles. The particles of these substances like to be in contact with each other. Air molecules can dissolve water molecules. We call that air humidity. A few carbon atoms can be dissolved in iron. We call that mild steel.

If we dissolve salt or sugar in water, single salt or sugar particles are surrounded by water. In this example, water is the solvent. Sugar/salt is the solute. Water can dissolve only a very specific amount of these particles. How much it can dissolve depends on these factors: Temperature, pressure, particle size and particle shape, and also on how many particles are already in the water. Sea water for example can dissolve less additional salt than tap water or distilled water. Solvents like water evaporates all the time, even at room temperature. The amount of solute (salt/sugar) in the mixture remains constant. There are fewer particles of water left, but the same amount of sugar particles. At some point, the solute (salt/sugar) crystals reappear. This point is called the solubility limit. We can stir harder and longer. The crystals will still not dissolve. The concentration of sugar has become too high. Water evaporation can be used to separate solvent and solute. It can also be used to grow crystals. Let's grow some cool crystals.

Sugar-Gro'

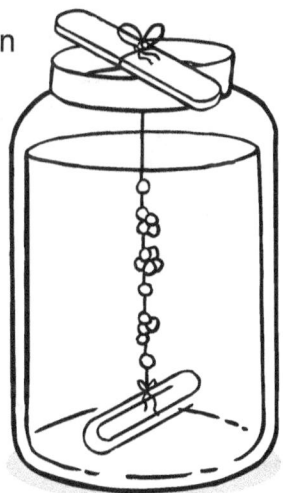

Objectives:
- Over-saturate water with salt or sugar
- Grow crystals from a salt solution and a sugar solution

Equipment:
- clear glass beaker or jam glass
- paper clip
- water (the solvent)
- 100 g of table salt (NaCl) or sugar (the solute)
- thread
- chopstick or popsicle stick
- heat source (for example hot plate)

Procedure:

1. Fill the glass container ¾ full with water.
2. Dissolve the solids (sugar or salt) in the water with sufficient stirring.
3. Heat up the water until it boils. Add one tablespoon of sugar (or salt) each minute while heating. Stir constantly. Keep on adding solids until you can see that they do not dissolve any more.
4. Remove the glass from the heater. Place it where it can stand undisturbed for one week.
5. Suspend a thread from a chopstick spanning the top of the glass. The thread can reach the bottom. Let the solution dry for one week. Keep the lid open.
6. The water will evaporate. At some point, there will be insufficient water. The sugar or salt can no longer be dissolved. The solute will start crystallizing. The thread has a rough irregular surface. It acts as a nucleation site. Most of the crystals will grow there. There will also be a crystal film on the glass.

Solu-what?

Worksheet

Explanation: Did you notice that more salt/sugar could be dissolved in hot water? That is true for most mixtures of liquids and solids. Some exceptions exist.

You could not dissolve any more salt/sugar in your liquid at some point? In this case, the solution is called "saturated." We cool such a saturated solution in this experiment. The dissolved salt/sugar cannot stay in solution. It will crystallize. It forms the solid white crystals we can see.

Take a look at the images below. The large particles are salt ions (sodium and chlorine). The small particles are water molecules.

Write under the image which one you think is :
1. Tap water
2. Water with less salt than can be dissolved
3. Water with salt crystallizing

1) Salt Molecule

2) Water Molecule

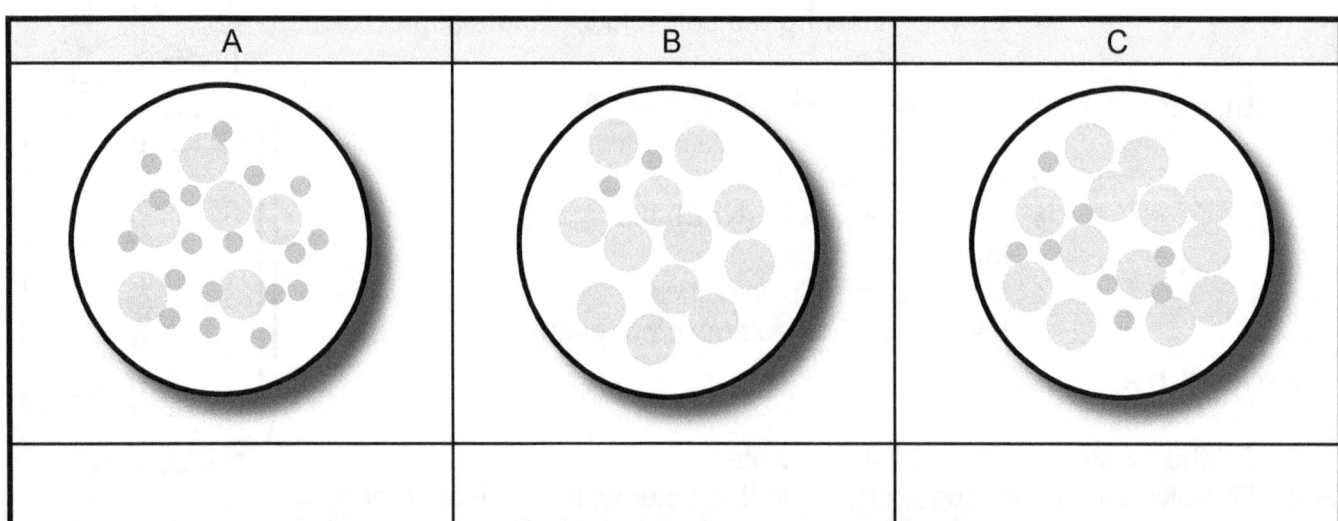

Cool Facts: When is a mixture a solution, when is it a colloid?

If you cannot distinguish between the phases by eye or microscope, the mixture is likely a solution. The dissolved material exists as single molecules. All molecules in a pinch of salt will dissolve in fresh tap water, but these molecules can also clump together into chunks. The mixture is then called a colloid. Milk is a colloid. The fat particles clump together. They make milk appear milky.

Solu-Solubility – A Poem

For solubility:
In Water, the source of life –
Alkali metals, ammonium salts,
Can always be depended on.
Whatever they may be.

Acetates and nitrates here:
The solution is so clear,
They each and all are dear -
And soluble in water,
That is what we like to hear.

The halogens now:
The bromides, chlorides, iodides
Are soluble. We read!
Save silver, mercury's low
And, of course, the halides of lead

And what about the sulfates:
They are soluble, it is said.
Except barium, mercury, strontium
That's not all:
And calcium and lead.

Some remain intact:
Sulfides and hydroxides
They do not dissolve at all
But barium, calcium, strontium,
Are partially soluble

And finally to tough ones:
The carbonates and phosphates
Insoluble – you must be pleased to hear
Or else, all our marble structures
Would surely wash away – and we would live in fear.

Extension (Creative Writing): If students are performing solubility experiments, such as the ones in this book, they can expand these poems themselves, based on the findings.

Dio-mio-Iodine:

Introducing the Concepts of Solvent and Solubility

This is a demo experiment, not for student use, and must be performed in a fume hood with the proper safety equipment.

Objective:

- Show solubility of iodine in different materials.

Equipment:

- CCl_4 (carbon tetrachloride, Dry Cleaner solvent)
- water
- ether
- graduated cylinder
- iodine crystals

Procedure:

1. In a fume-hood, carefully pour CCl_4, then water, then ether into the graduated cylinder.
2. Take care not to mix the materials, but to layer them.
3. Drop several crystals of iodine through the layers.
4. Prevent any movement of the cylinder.
5. Wait and observe the color in each layer.

Explanations: The solute in this case is iodine. The different liquids are the solvent. Some are more likely to dissolve the iodine ions than others. This is indicated by the color observed. CCl_4 will be purple, it dissolves the iodine better than the other liquids. You might observe that the liquid at the bottom, CCl_4, has an unfair advantage. It has more time to dissolve the iodine. Do experiments in separate cylinders. Each cylinder then only contains one solvent. Drop in the same amount of iodine into each. The result will be the same. Some of the smaller crystals can show some fast movements when they are at the interface between two different liquids. Note: CCl_4 can also be replaced with other organic solvents such as toluene or cyclohexane. All of these are toxic chemicals. The effect of dissolving iodine (purple color) can also simply be mentioned, and the experiment be carried out with only two phases: water and ether. You can also experiment with further mixtures such as water and oil.

Cool Facts: CCl_4 is commonly used as a coolant in fridges. It is also the most common dry cleaning solvent used extensively since the 1940's.

Dio-mio-Iodine

Solvent – Solubility Worksheet

In the graphics below, draw and color the different layers you observe before and after the iodine.

3 solvents before entering iodine	3 solvents after entering iodine

Based on these results, finish the following sentences.

1. Iodine crystals sink to the bottom of the cylinder, because they are _____ than all three liquids. (denser, less dense)

2. Iodine has _____ solubility in CCl_4 (or toluene). (higher, medium, low) That is indicated by the liquid becoming very darkly colored in the color of iodine ions.

3. Iodine has _____ solubility in ether. (high, medium, low) That is indicated by the liquid becoming brown, a weak version of the iodine ion coloration.

4. Iodine has _____ solubility water. (high, medium, low) That is indicated by the liquid remaining almost colorless.

Thus we can say that ….

5. … iodine molecules _____ (like, somewhat like, do not like) to be surrounded by CCl_4 molecules.

6. … iodine molecules _____ (like, somewhat like, do not like) to be surrounded by ether molecules.

7. … iodine molecules _____ (like, somewhat like, do not like) to be surrounded by water molecules.

We learned that not all particles are alike. Their differences can cause different behaviors in solubility.

They Live in the jungle

Let's grow a crystal jungle. We will utilize the fact that solvents can dissolve certain salts. These salts later re-form into crystals.

Objectives:

- Grow a crystal jungle.
- Observe the growth rate and crystal shape of different materials.

Equipment:

- sodium silicate solution (water glass)
- distilled water
- crystals of hydrated forms
- small jars or vials, covered or uncovered. If they have a tight lid, the gardens can be transported
- washed fine white sand
- various metal salts

The list below contains only some examples. Many other metals salts (mainly nitrates, chlorides and sulfates) work too. You can experiment with them. Observe safety protocols. Many of these chemicals are dangerous for humans on contact.

Metal Salt	Color	Metal Salt	Color
aluminum(III) chloride ($AlCl_3$)	white	copper(II) chloride ($CuCl_2$)	light blue-green
aluminum(III) nitrate $Al(NO_3)_3$	white	copper(II) sulfate ($CuSO_4$)	light blue
aluminum potassium sulfate $AlK(SO_4)_2 \cdot 12H_2O$	grayish	iron(III) chloride ($FeCl_3$)	yellow
chromium(III) chloride ($CrCl_3$)	dark green	iron(II) sulfate ($FeSO_4$)	grayish white
chromium(III) nitrate $Cr(NO_3)_3$	dark green	nickel(II) chloride ($NiCl_2$)	light green
cobalt(II) chloride ($CoCl_2$)	dark blue	nickel(II) sulfate ($NiSO_4$)	green
cobalt(II) nitrate $Co(NO_3)_2$	dark blue	tin chloride ($SnCl_4$)	white

Procedure:

1. Clean the glass thoroughly.
2. Enter the washed sand until the bottom is covered. This will provide a pleasing look. The sand is not involved in the reaction.
3. Pour sodium silicate into your container. Can be diluted with three parts distilled water.
4. Choose any of the salts you like. Handle all compounds with care.

They Live in the Jungle

5. Drop the crystals of the salts into the solution. Create your own patterns.
6. The reaction starts immediately. It will be mostly finished within minutes. However, allow it to continue one week without disturbing the container. The color of each column is determined by the salt crystal cation.
7. Once the garden has grown, you can either allow the solution to evaporate in a well ventilated place leaving a dry crystal garden. Or you can put a cap on the vial, and store it indefinitely.

Explanations:

Crystal salts are added to the sodium silicate solution. Colorful plant-like extensions grow from the surface of each crystal. From the standpoint of the particle theory, salts are a combination of two different types of particle. One is a cation. This can be a positively charged metal ion. The other is a negatively charged anion like chlorine. As both ions dissolve, the metal ions combine with silicate ions. They form membranes of insoluble silicates around the crystals. The inside of the membranes contains lower water concentrations and higher salt concentrations. That is why water passes inward by osmosis. This causes breaks in the membrane. Consequently, more membrane surface is formed. More metal ions dissolve in the water and expand the growing stalagmites.

Cool Facts: Table salt crystals were worth their weight in gold! That was during the time of the Roman Empire (ca. 2000 years ago).

If you keep the garden lid closed, the solution will become milky after many months. About one year later, the white material will precipitate. It will fall onto your crystal tree branches, looking like snow.

Draw three different crystal trees from your own crystal jungle. Imagine the line below as the bottom of your vial.

Salt 1:	Salt 2:	Salt 3:

Do-It-Yourself Precious Gemstones

Ever heard of malachite? Or, more to the point: copper carbonate hydroxide (the same thing, different name)? In any case, here's an experiment where you can make the precious greenish gem yourself. All you need is an empty egg shell and some chemicals. There goes "ye' good olde" painted Easter egg and out comes a "Gemstone" egg!

Objective:

- Create malachite from calcium carbonate

Equipment:

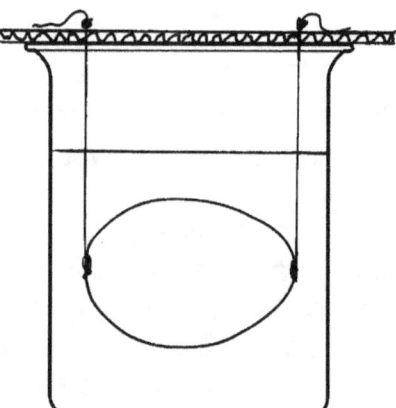

- Calcium-carbonate containing material (e.g. a blown-out egg shell, shellfish shell, some stones like lime or marble)
- Copper sulfate solution ($CuSO_4$). This can be purchased as blue vitriol which is fully hydrated blue $CuSO_4 \times 5\ H_2O$.
- Glass or vial large enough to fit around the egg shell (Beaker suggested, a jam jar is also great, but never ever use it for food again afterwards)
- Metal wire or woolen thread
- Chopstick (alternatively a skewer, or cardboard piece – these will be put over your beaker and will hold the egg with the help of the thread)
- Acetone or nail polish remover for cleaning the egg shells (optional)
- Tweezers and clinging foils as a lid

Procedure:

1. Take an egg. Any bird's egg (or clam shell) will do. Punch small holes on both sides. Blow it out. You can use the contents to make scrambled eggs, or use it in a cake.

2. Then, make a little holder for the egg shell using a wire system. You can suspend it from the edges of the container rim. Or punch two holes in a cardboard and knot it around those holes. Test your setup in the empty glass. See that your holder will hold the egg shell. Also take care that the shell does not touch any of the edges, or the bottom.

3. Now wash the shell thoroughly without breaking it. Use acetone (nail polish remover) without touching it. Do this in a well ventilated place. This will remove all fats and lipids that were on the egg, including your fingerprints. If this is not done, there will be areas on the egg that will be protected against gemstone creation. You can also use this method to paint something on the egg with a marker. It will create a relief in your product later.

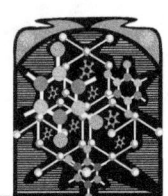

Do-It-Yourself Precious Gemstones

4. Now, let's make the blue stuff. If you have $CuSO_4$ as a crystalline powder, dissolve it in water. If you use more powder, you will have a higher concentration. The color of your product will change. As a guideline, you can use approximately 10-20g of vitriol in 250 ml water, but you can experiment! Don't fill your container more than ¾ full. The egg volume still has to fit in. Place the container where it can stand undisturbed for months. Put a saucer under it that can contain any liquid that might leak for safety purposes.

5. Carefully enter the egg into the solution using tweezers. If the holes you punched into the eggs are small, it will take a long time to fill its inside with solution. Be patient. The egg is very buoyant when empty. It must be fully immersed.

6. In order to reduce the loss of liquid water due to evaporation, put a lid of clinging foil on your glass. You can add water, if too much evaporates. Take care not to drip. And don't perturb the gem growth by moving the glass. Take a look at the egg first once a day, later once a week. Note the changes on the surface. You can raise it out of the solution, too, to check its color, but the growth will be disturbed then. Sometimes, white spiky crystals are formed on the surface, too. That depends on how warm, sunny and dry the storage space is, and how often it is perturbed.

Explanations: The solution helps in the removal of the calcium ions (Ca_{2+}) from the surface of the shell. The calcium ions are then replaced by the copper ions (Cu_{2+}).

Ion? Like in the Starship Enterprise? Correct. Ion just means this is an atom which misses (or has too many) electrons. In this case, both copper and calcium are cations. Cations are positively charged. If you can't remember that, dig this: "Cation" has a "t", which looks like a plus. t = +. Positive charge. Metal ions are usually cations.

A thin film of azurite is formed on the egg shell within hours. Azurite's chemical structure looks like this: $Cu_3(CO_3)_2(OH)_2$. Within a matter of days, this blue stuff is then converted into green stuff. This is malachite, $Cu_2CO_3(OH)_2$.

Cool Fact: Calcium is present in egg shells and bones. **Wait a minute, I also have calcium in my teeth!** Correct. We remove material from our teeth when we drink pop or fruit juices. That can weaken our teeth. In fact, pop often contains acids as additives. The best drink to sustain good, healthy teeth is tap water. Water also contains minerals which are good for teeth and bones. For example, calcium!

Do-It-Yourself Precious Gemstones

Cool Facts: Blue azurite was ground and used to paint blue skies in oil paintings. There, like in our egg, it undergoes the slow transformation to malachite. This can take many decades. But the images might have been painted in the 1800s. That is why the paintings using this pigment all have a greenly tinted sky now.

Copper? Isn't that, like, worth a lot? Indeed. We require fuels to extract metals and transport them. Due to the continuing price hike in oil prices and the economic growth in Asia, metal prices are on the rise. More and more humans live on this planet. All want more goods. Less and less oil is actually available. This trend will probably accelerate over the next decades. In North America, there are strong economic arguments for removing the penny altogether from circulation. This would free tons of valuable copper.

Extensions (Geology, Igneous Stones): If you use feldspar or quartz instead, what happens? Nothing. These stones are not as easily attacked by acidic solutions, and do not exchange their ions with copper. Eggs, limestone, marble, and carbonate-containing stones will bubble and fizzle when concentrated acid is poured on them. They emit carbon dioxide gas. This is a nice introduction to rock formation, and the chemical differences in the rocks that are found all around us.

Use the space below to write notes about your egg's color, crystal, shape, temperature and water level

Day 1: _____

Day 2: _____

Day 3: _____

Day 4: _____

Day 5: _____

Week 2: _____

Week 4: _____

Week 6: _____

Week 8: _____

Tensing Surfaces

Liquid/Gas Interfaces

Whenever there are interfaces between materials, there are surfaces. Each particle of a substance likes to be surrounded by particles of the same substance. But on a surface the particles are only partially surrounded by their own kind. Every system consequently tries to reduce its surface. This creates surface tension. Some of these surfaces are clearly defined. The most common surface is the one we all stand on: earth. Another common surface is the one between water and air. The surface tension can be observed by the eye. It can even be changed with chemicals.

Objective:
- Change the surface tension of water.

Equipment:
- empty glass
- soap
- water
- paper clip
- fork

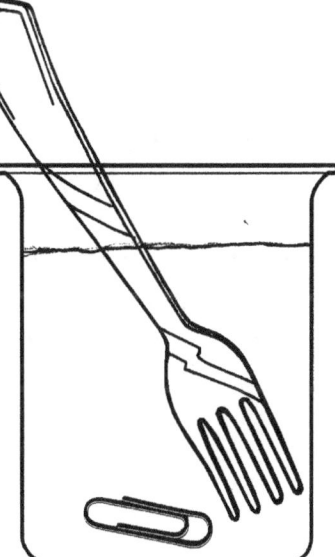

Procedure:

1. Fill the glass with water to 1cm below the rim.
2. Drop a paper clip into the water. Observe how it drops through the interface. It will sink.
3. Use a fork. Carefully lower one paper clip onto the surface. It will float. This is tricky and may take a little while.
4. Add a drop of soap. The surface tension will be lowered. Soap makes water and air "like" each other more. The paper clip will sink.

Cool Facts: Can you fill more water into a container than it will fit? Yes! The surface tension will allow for slightly more liquid to be stored in the container. The water bulges above the rim.

Fill in the following text by completing the words:

Every matter surface has surface t _ _ _ _ _ _ _. In the case of a water-air surface, this tension is h _ _ _. The surface tension between m _ _ _ _ _ _ y and air is even higher. This toxic liquid metal does not like to be around air. The surface tension can be l _ _ _ _ _ _ when soap is added. Some animals use the surface tension of water as a walk-able surface. They are called water _ _ _ _ _ _ _ _ s. They _ _ _ k when the surface tension vanishes.

Un-tensing Surfaces

Objective: ♦ Record the change in surface tension of different liquids

Equipment:
♦ paper
♦ liquid soap
♦ ballpoint pen
♦ other liquids (e.g. juice, ethanol, glue, oil)
♦ water
♦ chemical dropper or pipette (optional)

Procedure:
1. Copy this page.
2. Put a single drop of liquid on the paper in the box below. You can use a pencil or chemical dropper to transfer the drop.
3. Draw the drop diameter with a pen.
4. Add soap to the liquid.
5. Put a single drop of liquid soap in another box.
6. Measure and compare the diameters.
7. Draw conclusions.

Water droplet	Water & soap droplet	Other liquid (_____) droplet	Other liquid (_____) plus soap droplet
Diameter (in or mm): _____	Diameter (in or mm): _____	Diameter (in or mm): _____	Diameter (in or mm): _____

Conclusion:

1. The diameter of the water droplet is _____ (smaller, larger, the same) as the diameter of the water droplet with soap.

2. The surface tension of pure water is _____ (lowered, increased, staying the same) when you add soap.

3. The diameter of the liquid droplet is _____ (smaller, larger, the same) as the diameter of the liquid droplet with soap.

© On The Mark Press • S&S Learning Materials OTM-2137 • SSB1-137 The Nature of Matter

Bubble-icious:

Soap Bubbles Follow Precise Mathematical Equations!

Objectives:
- Produce soap bubbles
- Record their shape and interaction

Equipment:
- dish washing detergent
- a straw
- water
- pipe cleaners (bent into a ring; these can make large bubbles)
- cups for solutions and plates (optional) for making the bubbles on

Procedure:

1. One day before bubble making, mix one part dish detergent with 10 parts soft water.
2. Spread on a flat surface (for example a table or plate).
3. Blow bubbles on the table or plate using a straw.
4. Create bubbles inside bubbles. Observe the change in volume when blowing up the inner bubble. Both bubbles will increase since the inner volume pushes away the outer.
5. Combine bubbles by pulling together several bubbles of similar size. Draw the wall patterns that you create in the boxes below. Try to create bubbles of equal sizes. Draw a top view image of the bubbles and their interfaces.
6. Shape pipe cleaners to a ring. A triangle. In heart shape. Does that influence the bubble shape?

1 bubble	2 bubbles	3 bubbles	4 bubbles
5 bubbles	6 bubbles	7 bubbles	8 bubbles

My bubbles started having one central bubble with _____ walls once I combined more than _____ bubbles to one structure.

Cool Facts: The reason that soap bubbles burst is two-fold. One reason is they dry out and the second reason is they lose liquid. In an experiment, try inserting a wet versus a dry straw. Catch bubbles with a wet versus a dry hand. They burst when they come in contact with dry materials. This has nothing to do with sharpness of the materials!

Mixing Oil and Water

Liquid/Liquid Interfaces

Some liquids can be mixed. Their particles like to be in contact with each other. Alcohol and water is such a case. Other liquids do not mix. These particles do not want to be surrounded by each other. Oil and water for example. Washing in pure water barely cleans oily dirt from clothes. The oil sticks to the fabric. However, oil and water can be mixed with a trick. We can use soap. Soap particles have two sides. One side likes contact with water, the other with oil. Oil droplets are surrounded by a "skin" of soap. The other side of the soap particle is in contact with water. In this way, the soap pulls the oil from the clothes. Our clothes are thus cleaned.

Objectives:
- Observe miscibility of oil and water.
- Observe the effect of soap on this liquid/liquid interface.

Materials:
- soap
- vegetable oil (for example, sunflower oil)
- water
- beaker or transparent cylinder or jam jar with a lid (10-50ml)

Procedure:

1. Pour water into the jar.
2. Add a thin layer of oil (less than 1cm).
3. Mix them vigorously (with a finger or by closing the lid and shaking).
4. Let the mix settle for a minute. Observe changes.
5. Add soap to the mix, at least half as much as oil.
6. Repeat the mixing.
7. Wait and observe. If materials still separate, add more soap.

Fill in the text below:

When mixing oil and water, they _____ (separate, stay mixed). The oil is _____ (below, on top of) the water. Water has a _____ (lower, higher) density than oil. Water and oil particles _____ (like, don't like) to be in contact with each other.

If we add soap to a mixture of oil and water, the mixture _____ (separates, stays mixed). Soap particles _____ (like, don't like) to be in contact with water. They _____ (like, don't like) to be in contact with oil. Soap particles _____ (separate from, squeeze between) oil and water particles.

Muddy Hell! The Science of Soil Erosion

Liquid/Solid Mixtures

Separating solids and liquids is relatively straightforward. We can sieve the solids out. This happens in nature, too. Imagine the roots of trees as gigantic sieves. They "sieve out" the solid particles like earth and allow the water to pass. That is why the rich, healthy soil accumulates in our forests. Once the forests have been removed, the trees are dead or gone. The sieve is no longer in place. Water and soil will swim away together. This is called erosion.

Humans have started to deforest our planet on a large scale. Often, forest is burned to make space for cattle farms. The soil is no longer held in place by vegetation. It gets washed away. What remains are dead rock surfaces. We can simulate this in the classroom.

Objectives:
- How does vegetation stabilize soil?
- What are some different run-off processes?
- How does forestry and land use affect water quality and flood timing?

Equipment:
- graduated cylinder or measuring cup (1L)
- 30 small cups with exact ml measurement units (3x numbered 1-10)
- large aluminum roasting tray (one per soil sample)
- different soil samples: sod (collect leftovers from edging the lawns and let it grow together for 2 weeks), soil with roots (can be freshly collected on the day), beach or playground sand
- timer

Procedure:

1. Designate a timer, a cup provider, a cup holder, and a cup taker in your group.

2. Set the soil into the aluminum tray. Incline it. Start the "rainstorm" by slowly pouring water onto the high end of the soil. Hold an empty cup under the hole which is at the lower end.

3. The timer starts to time at the beginning of the rainstorm. She/He calls "Switch" every 10 seconds. The cup holder collects the water coming out of the tray. The cups are switched every 10 seconds. The cup provider makes sure the holder has a fresh cup ready. The cup taker takes the cups and stores them safely. If only a couple of drips every 10 seconds come out of the tray, stop the experiment.

4. Fill in the table. Then plot the time in 10 second intervals along the bottom axis of a graph, and the volume in ml along the y-axis.

Muddy Hell! The Science of Soil Erosion

Worksheet

Time (seconds)	Sod Volume (ml)	Fresh soil with roots Volume (ml)	Beach sand Volume (ml)
10			
20			
30			
40			
50			
60			
70			
80			
90			
100			
110			
120			
130			
140			
150			
160			
170			
180			
190			
200			

A Little Fizz to Freeze

Liquid/Gas Mixture

Objectives:
- Cool a bottle of carbonated drink. It should remain liquid even below the freezing point of water.
- Open it and see the whole bottle freezing shut at once.

Equipment:
- small transparent plastic bottle of unopened fizzy (carbonated) drink; remove the label for better viewing
- bowl full of ice
- water
- salt
- thermometer

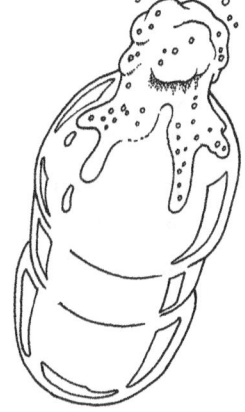

Procedure:

1. Add water and ice into the bowl. The ice should be half covered in water.
2. Add several spoons of salt to the ice mixture.
3. Measure the temperature, it should be at least -4°C (30°F) cold.
4. Bury the drink bottle in the ice mixture.
5. Wait about 20 to 30 minutes. If the drink freezes, you have waited too long. Restart with a fresh bottle.
6. The same can be done in a freezer. Figure out how long the drink needs to start freezing. Take the bottle out one minute before that happens.
7. Open the bottle and observe. Can get messy.
8. The contents of the bottle should turn to slush in front of your eyes.

Explanations: Before opening the bottle of carbonated liquid, it contains high quantities of carbon dioxide (CO_2). The gas is dissolved in the liquid. This reduces the freezing point. That is the same effect that salt has on ice. That is why the salt-water mixture is below the freezing point of water. The drink does not freeze even at -3°C (31°F). When opening the bottle, the dissolved carbon-dioxide is released. This increases the freezing point of the liquid. It also creates lots of little bubbles. The liquid is now colder than its freezing point. It starts freezing. The freeze process would still take a long time, but many small bubbles are also created. They act as crystallization nuclei.

Cool Facts: Freezing a material creates heat. Liquids have to be sufficiently cold to still be below freezing point after crystallization. Otherwise, the liquid remains in its liquid phase, even after opening the bottle. The heating effect of crystallization can be clearly felt in the case of chemical handwarmers.

Smoking Mirrors

Gas/Solid Mixtures

Objectives:

- Understand how air cleaners work.

Equipment:

- Bunsen burner or candle
- ceramic plate

Description:

Turn the Bunsen burner to a yellow (low temperature) flame or use a candle. This flame is not fully burning the fuel gas and produces soot. Soot is mainly carbon. This also happens in each of our cars. These particles are dangerous when inhaled. That's why we have to scrub the exhausts of factories and why we have to install soot traps and catalysts into our car exhaust streams. Hold the ceramic plate above the flame. It cools the hot air stream from the flame. The carbon particles adsorb (get stuck) on its surface. It separates gas and solid.

Here is space for you to draw and label the experiment.

Drawing:

Notes:_____
_____
_____
_____
_____

Extensions (Chemistry, Engineering): Novel alternative energy systems do not need gasoline. They can run on a gas called hydrogen. One such system is a fuel cell. Hydrogen fuel storage is difficult. Hydrogen molecules are very small, but they can be stored within a metal. The metal acts as foam for the hydrogen and forms solid metal hydrides. When temperature and pressure are changed, the hydrogen is released again as gas.

The Needle in the Haystack

How to Separate Mixtures

Many substances only mix physically. They do not react chemically to a new material. These mixtures can be separated. Let's perform some physical separations.

Objectives:
- Physically separate different solids.

Equipment:
- water
- glass marbles
- magnets
- beakers
- salt
- nails
- tweezers
- heat source
- sieve
- flour
- toothbrush
- coffee filters
- sugar
- bath salts
- food coloring
- chalk
- magnifying glass
- tea leaves

Description:

You have the following mixtures of solids:

1. tea leaves and sugar
2. salt and flour
3. chalk powder and bath salts
4. salt, glass marbles, nails and tea leaves
5. sand, styrofoam granules and soap

How can you separate these mixtures?

Cool Facts: Many liquid colors that we see are mixtures of other colors. Green food coloring is often a mixture of blue and yellow. Colors and other chemicals in a solution can be separated. One such separation technique is chromatography. It is easy to do this yourself. Mix less than a teaspoon of salt with four cups of water. Make a color dot on the lower end of a coffee filter. Hang the bottom edge of the filter into your salt water. Do not disturb the filter. Wait and observe the result.

The Needle in the Haystack

How to Separate Mixtures

Materials can be separated based on their physical properties. Many powders and dry leaves float on water. Salt and sugar dissolve in water. They crystallize into solids once the water evaporates. Glass marbles sink in water. They have a higher density. Most metals are magnetic. They are pulled out of a mix with a magnet. Some materials are flammable. Glass decorations hidden in a candle can be revealed by burning the wax. Also, differently sized grains are separated by differently sized sieves. Experiment with different materials. Find out about their properties. Write down your findings here. The first one is already done for you.

Material	Your Findings
salt	Can be sieved. Dissolves in water. Does not float. Is not magnetic.
dry tea leaves	
sugar	
chalk powder	
glass marbles	
needles	
flour	
food coloring	

Cool Facts: Some matter can be separated by freezing. Gases with different boiling and freezing points are separated by cooling them. The gases with the highest boiling points will precipitate first.

Answer Key

Matter matters. What's the matter? (Page 17)
Gas - Carbon Dioxide,
Liquid - Coca Cola,
Solid - Stone

Matter Matters. Matter Around You (Page 19)

material	is it hard or soft?	is it light or heavy?	can you see it?	does it change its form on touch it?	what matter do you think this is?
balloon	soft	light	yes	yes	gas (inside) solid (skin)
your hand	soft outside, hard inside	light	yes	yes	solid outside, some liquid inside
water	soft	heavy (depends on perception of heavy)	yes	yes	liquid
chalk	hard	light	yes	no	solid
breath	soft	light	no	yes	gas
find more yourself					

Let's Get Some Heat - Worksheet (Page 22)
1. Water freezes under STP (standard temperature and pressure).
2. At the solid/liquid transition.
3. Water boils under STP (standard temperature and pressure).
4. At the liquid/gas phase transition.

Hot Calculations (Page 23)
a) Never, b) -40, c) -614.5 – can never be reached, d) 574.59, e) Never, f) 0
More scales, for example:
Rømer scale: ([°C]= [°Rø] - 7.5) × 40/21),
Réaumur scale: ([°C]= [°Ré] × 5/4)
Temperature calculations done at sea level: Depending on the pressure, the freezing and boiling points of matter changes. For discussions, see teachers notes (p.21).

The Pressure Worksheet (Page 25)
Answers will vary.

Rise and Shine Worksheet (Page 27)
1. Observe the changes in boiling temperature. Lower pressure, lower boiling point.
2. Higher pressure – higher boiling point, Lower pressure – lower boiling point.
3. More particles in the air, pressing the particles in the water back into itself. They cannot escape (boil). Thus, higher boiling point.
4. Potatoes take longer to become soft. Water boils at lower temperature. Some food might never be fully cooked.

The Matter Game - Worksheet (Page 29)
1. Strong interaction forces in solids
2. Heat – Thermal energy of a system = expressed in high velocities of the molecules
3. Increase in energy – Melting, Evaporation
4. Increase p.
5. Metallic (electron cloud), Ionic (NaCl, +/- attraction), Covalent (e.g. diamond), Van-der-Walls (weak H-H bonds, present in most organic molecules and water)

Mass Volume Density (Page 30)
1.-4. Answers will vary. 5: No, tubes had always the same shape, 6: 50g, 50cm³, 1g/cm³, 7: float, 8: Ships have larger volume than that of the water displaced, but the same weight. Total density of the entire ship volume of air and metal is lower than that of the water.

Oily Icing (Page 32)
1. a) 2. b) 3. a) 4. a)

Just Hot Gas Worksheet (Page 34)
1. Stretching the polymer allows it to be more flexible and expand even if only a little gas is produced.
2. Gas expands when heated. Hot air has a lower density than ambient air. Since the weight and the volume of the bottle remain constant, the volume increases outward into the balloon. We do not create more air, and there is no influence due to water vapor!
3. They start moving faster. That is what heat is. More movement creates more pressure. Thus the balloon expands.
4. No. We do not create more air.
5. Cold air contracts.
6. They move slower. Less movement – less pressure. The balloon deflates.

Press it! (Page 35)

Material	State	Compressible/Not Compressible
Stone	Solid	No
Water	Liquid	No
Gas	Gaseous	Yes

The Swirl of Hot Color (Page 37)
The drawings should indicate that color diffuses faster in warmer water.
1. Hot liquid. More convection currents, faster diffusion. More energy.
2. Even faster diffusion and mixing due to bubbles.
3. No. Ice is a solid. Diffusion through a solid takes a very long time.

Some Honey, Honey? Worksheets (Pages 40-41)
1. a) The straw barely changes shape. b) The straw collapses on itself.
2. Ice cream is more viscous, because the straw contracts.
5. Honey is more viscous than oil and oil more viscous than water (depending on type of honey and oil as well as temperature), because the marble drops more slowly.
7. Honey is more viscous, because the force it took to shear two sheets was highest. (Can be oil too, if a very viscous oil at room temperature is chosen)

Let's Get Changed Worksheet (Page 44)
Exchanges Between States Worksheet. Some examples (others are possible, depending on pressure selected). Further notes for the teacher: All gases follow ideal gas law. Pressure times volume equals amount of molecules times temperature (times a constant called ideal gas constant R), $pV=nT*R$.

1. **Solid -> Liquid:** Ice Melting (Water, T=273.15K, p=1 atm)
2. **Sold -> Liquid:** CCl_4 Melting (CCl_4, T=250K, p=1 atm)
3. **Solid -> Gaseous:** CO_2 Sublimation (CO_2, T=194.5K, p=1 atm)
4. **Liquid -> Solid:** CO_2 solidification from liquid (CO_2, T=225K, p=7 atm (must be >5))
5. **Liquid -> Gaseous:** Iron Evaporation (Iron, T=3023.15 K, p=1atm)
6. **Gaseous -> Solid:** Graphite deposition from gas phase (C, T= 4098K, p=1atm)
7. **Gaseous -> Liquid:** Nitrogen liquefaction (N_2, T=123K, p=1atm)

Creating Clouds 1 and 2 Worksheet (Page 47)
1. decreases 2. water 3. more 4. single water molecules 5. suck in 6. help with 7. can (if air is cold enough)

The Cloud Game Worksheet (Page 49)
1. Particle Theory dictates that more molecules in the gas phases means increased pressure on the liquid surface. This forces more water molecules from the gas phase into the water. It is like pressing a tooth paste tube.
2. Many water molecules are suddenly released from the water into the gas phase.
3. Soot particles act as condensation nuclei.

Slightly Sublime Worksheet (Page 51)
1. Ice slowly sublimates without liquefaction, so given enough time, the clothes will be dry, assuming a reasonably stable temperature.
2. The weight changes. In dry conditions, it decreases. Also, some weight might be lost if the towel gets too warm and melts some of the ice onto the balance.
3. Sublimation of water in the freezer or outdoors.
4. Use different media (meat) or bread, or a different liquid than water, if it can be frozen in the freezer. Do not put chemicals into a freezer together with edible foods.
5. While the food is as safe as food protected from desiccation in the freezer, the taste of the denatured food might be off. However, as opposed to bacteriological infestations, the bad part can simply be cut out.

CO_2 Fun (Pages 52)
Observations: Both systems bubble and produce vapor. But only one is a hot system (water evaporation as steam), the other is a cold system (water condensation). In hot water, the gas produced is gaseous water (not hydrogen or oxygen). The bubbles produced by dry ice in water are carbon dioxide.

CO_2 Fun Worksheet (Pages 53-54)
1. False. Temperature only increases once the ice is gone.
2. True. The ice cube's core was likely below zero. This is measurable if a thermometer is frozen into the ice in advance. This might crack the thermometer, though.
3. False. Cannot decrease while heating.
4. True.
5. False. Will become clear with a graph.
6. False. Water cannot be hotter than 100°C at STP.
7. True. Steam can be hotter than 100°C. It can even ignite paper.

Drawings on page 54: Warm water: Many bubbles. Cold water: Only a few bubbles and a thin ice sheet around the dry ice.

8. Warm water: faster sublimation of CO_2 – more gas created in a shorter time – more bubbles.
9. The water approaches 0°C. Dry ice starts to form a crust of frozen ice. This can encapsulate the CO_2 cube, until the pressure inside increases so much that it pops open.
10. No. Although we see bubbles as if the water is boiling, it is not boiling. It only bubbles due to CO_2 release.
11. The ice can encapsulate the CO_2 cube, until the pressure inside increases so much that it pops open. Also, if moved to a warmer water bath, the vigorous bubbling will resume.
12. The white vapor is actually water. It is not boiled out of the water, not even part of, or coming from the water bath. The gas coming off the frozen CO_2 is CO_2, a colorless, odorless gas. Since it is cold, it condenses the water FROM THE AIR and thus forms vapor. Hot, boiling gas rises (lower density), cold gas sinks (higher density).
13. The steam is really vapor not steam, and it sinks, showing that the gas (CO_2) has a higher density than air, and thus sinks to the bottom. Also, it cools the air which also increases the density of air. This cooling effect though is less significant. It would be an insufficient explanation. Cold helium, for example, would still be likely to rise in room temperature air (depending on relative temperature).
14. Flames are extinguished since the CO_2 does not further oxidation and replaces all oxygen since it is heavier. This is not due to the vapor, but the CO_2.
15. CO_2 is heavier than air and, at some point, the density of the soap bubble (soap plus normal air blown into it) will be equal to the density of the CO_2 surrounding the air-filled bubble.

Chemical Creation of Gases and Heat Worksheet (Page 61)
Description: H_2O_2 decomposes quickly into water and oxygen in the presence of a catalyst. The additional gas (oxygen) inflates the balloon. Metal oxides can be catalysts for this reaction.
1. Oxygen – it increases the glow of a glow stick, but does not explode. Hydrogen is not produced, it falls out as water, bound with oxygen.
2. Cleaning stores (kills bacteria), hair dye (removes or destroys all color molecules in hair)
3. Hydrogen peroxide (using a catalyst) creates water and oxygen.
4. It is a catalyst, speeding up the reaction that would otherwise still occur, but over the course of weeks.
5. Depends on the oxide. Some oxides, like MnO, (green) might be further oxidized to MnO_2 (black), which is a change visible with the eye. Others are already in a higher oxidation state or require elevated temperatures to get into a higher state, or do not change color. In most cases, however, the metal oxide powder only supplies a large reactive surface area, whilst it remains unchanged (catalysts usually do not change during a reaction)
6. No. More catalyst means more reactive surface area and therefore a faster reaction. The amount of oxygen produced remains unchanged.
7. Yes. See 6 for explanation.
8. Yes. More hydrogen peroxide forms more oxygen.

React-it Worksheet (Page 63)
It turns out that most nails are not stainless steel and they will rust under these conditions. The bare metal rusts most. The others rust depending on how protective the layer we applied is. Usually a thick layer of Vaseline is more protective than a thin layer of paint. But that depends on the type and density of the paint. These layers prevent access of ions. Iron becomes a small battery in water. It forms localized ions of different valence, both starting and accelerating its chemical degradation.

Mix it, Shake it - Separate it. Worksheet (Page 70)
1. liquid/liquid: water and oil.
2. solid/gaseous: soot and air.
3. liquid/gaseous: water and air.
4. gaseous/liquid: CO_2 and water.
5. solid/liquid: cells and water.
6. liquid/solid: oil and sand
7. Answers will vary

Solu-what? Worksheet (Page 72)
Water molecules are drawn here much smaller than salt molecules. Their electron shells are much closer to the core. Also, in reality, there is significantly more water present. Even many solid crystals may contain water in their atomic structure.
a. 1), b. 3), c. 2)

One exception for lower solubility at higher temperatures is cerium sulfate in water. Also, strictly speaking, the "shape" of the molecule determines its polarity (charge imbalance). Water is polar, the electrons agglomerate on one side of the water molecule. This generates a weak dipole. Fats are usually unpolar. This effect determines their miscibility. Unpolar and polar molecules do not mix, as can be seen in oil/water experiments (e.g. p.84).

Solu-Solubility - A Poem (Page 73)
This poem, an adaptation from Ref 35, includes the proper names for many chemicals and relates them to their solubility properties. For higher grades, poems could, for example, use the crystal gardens (page 77) as inspiration.

Dio-mio-Iodine Solvent – Solubility Worksheet (Page 75)
1. denser 2. high 3. medium 4. low 5. like, 6. somewhat like 7. do not like

Tensing Surfaces (Page 81)
tension, high, mercury, lowered, skippers, sink

Un-tensing Surfaces (Page 82)
1. smaller, lowered 2. Depends on liquid chosen. Usually surfactant increase wetting and diameter.

Bubble-icious (Page 83)
No influence of pipe cleaner shape.
Physical Explanation: Bubbles are always spherical. A sphere has the smallest ratio of surface to volume. Similar-sized bubbles will share straight (planar) walls.

Mixing Oil and Water (Page 84)
separate, on top of, higher, don't like, stays mixed, like, like, squeeze between

Muddy Hell! the Science of Soil Erosion (Page 86)

Vegetation stabilizes the soil by spreading a network of roots. These hold together stones, finer sand and organic sod. This is similar to a sieve. Without a sieve, the solids would just flow away. In a sieve, everything is held in place.
With more roots and organic stuff present, water falling on the surface is held in place longer. The soil acts like a sponge. with playground/beach sand, the water flows off much faster. Also, more sand particles are washed away with the water.

Excessive logging, especially commercial cut-and-burn practices, kill all plant life capable of holding soil in place. The results are increased erosion, especially of the once-fertile sods. This necessitates new cuts to get to fresh fertile soil. Remaining soils often barely hold plant life.

The Needle in the Haystack (Page 90)

Material	Your Findings
salt	Can be sieved. Dissolves in water. Does not float. Is not magnetic.
dry tea leaves	Can be sieved. Will float until wet.
sugar	Can be sieved. Dissolves in water. Does not float. Is not magnetic.
chalk powder	Too fine for standard sieves. Floats for some time. Does not dissolve in water.
glass marbles	Sink in water and do not dissolve. Can be sieved easily.
nails	Are magnetic.
flour	Too fine for most kitchen sieves, unless wholemeal. Does not dissolve in water. However, water gets absorbed in it. The mixture is then called dough.
food color	Dissolves in water. Can be separated further into base colors by chromatography.
sand	Has a higher density than water. Sinks to the bottom. Sand can have different grain sizes than other materials and can be sieved out.
styrofoam granules	Have low density. Float on water.
soap	Dissolves in water. Can be recovered through evaporation of water.

Bibliography:

1) Alder, A., et al.: Introduction to Chemistry, Usborne Publishing Ltd., UK, (1983).
2) Barber, N., Keegan, T.: More Fun with Science. Experiments, Tricks, Things to Make, Grisewood and Dempsey, UK, (1989).
3) Bates, J.C. (Ed.): The Winston Primary Dictionary for Canadian Schools, Holt, Rinehart and Winston of Canada Limited. Toronto, ON, (1966).
4) Bosak, S.V.: Science is…, A Source Book of Fascinating Facts, Projects and Activities, 2nd Ed., Scholastic Canada Ltd., ON, (1991).
5) Cahande, D., Fisher, T.C.G.: Have a Penny? Need a Penny? Eliminating the One-Cent Coin from Circulation, Canadian Public Policy / Analyse de Politiques, Vol. 29, No. 4, pp. 511-517, (2003).
6) Dagnelie, P.C., Dusseldorp, M.V. et al: Effects of macrobiotic diets on linear growth in infants and children until 10 years of age. European Journal of Clinical Nutrition, 48, Suppl. 1, S103–S111, (1994).
7) Diu, B., et al.: The Lower End of the Sublimation Curve, European Journal of Physics. Vol. 23 No. 2: pp. 205-212, (2002).
8) Douglas, V.F. et al.: Experiments You Can Do in Your Kitchen Grades 5-8, McGraw Hill Children's Publishing, Columbus, OH, (2004).
9) Douglas, V.F. et al.: Wild & Wacky Science Experiments Grades 5-8, McGraw Hill Children's Publishing, Columbus, OH, (2004).
10) Faraday, M.: Faraday's Chemical History of a Candle: Twenty-Two Experiments and Six Classic Lectures, 1st Ed., Chicago Review Press, (1988).
11) Ford, L.A.: Chemical Magic, Dover Publications Inc., (1993).
12) Goddard, J.: Will Canada go Penny-less?, The Politics eZine – Economics, Bank's penny-less thoughts, Federal draft report says, unofficially, inflationary effect would be negligible, February 17th, (2007).
13) Herr, N.: Hands-On Chemistry Activities with Real-Life Applications: Easy-to-Use Labs and Demonstrations for Grades 8-12, Jossey-Bass Inc., (1999).
14) Kiseleva, I.A., Ogorodova, L.P., et al: Thermodynamic properties of copper carbonates - malachite and azurite, Physics and Chemistry of Minerals, Vol.19[5], December, (1992).
15) Kenda, M., Williams, P.S.: Science Wizardry for Kids, Barron's Educational Series, NY, (1992).
16) Kendall, H.: Stepping Stones to Science: True Tales and Awesome Activities, Teacher Ideas Press, (1997).
17) Kramer, A.: How to Make a Chemical Volcano: And Other Mysterious Experiments, Franklin Watts Inc. (1991).
18) Leonard, A.: The Story of Stuff: A complete Global Life Cycle Analysis, www.storyofstuff.com, (2008).
19) MacKenzie, K.: Watershed Activity - How does vegetation affect the quality and amount of water going into our streams?, http://ubclts.com/activityideas, BC, (2004).
20) Meloan, C.E.: Chemical Separations: Principles, Techniques and Experiments, Wiley-Interscience, (1999).
21) Millan, D.J.: Wheat or Meat for the Next Millenium? Proceedings of the Nutrition Society, 58, pp. 209–210, (1999)
22) Murphy, P., Klages, E., et al: The Science Explorer, Henry Holt Co., NY, (1996).

23) Murphy, P., Klages, E., et al: The Science Explorer Out and About, Henry Holt Co., NY, (1997).
24) O'Connor: Chemistry: Experiments and Principles, Laboratory Manual, Copp Clarke Co., Toronto ON, (1986).
25) Paull, J, Paull, D.: Basic Knowledge Chemistry, Ladybird Books Ltd., UK, (1989).
26) Pollan, M.: The Omnivore's Dilemma: A Natural History of Four Meals, Penguin Press HC, April 11, (2006).
27) Roesky, H.W.: Spectacular Chemical Experiments, Wiley-VCH (2007).
28) Rose, L.: Malachite Easter Egg – A student's experiment, Saugfinger, ISSN 1610-2665, Vol 2002 Iss. 1, pp.30, (2002).
29) Rose, L.: Father and Daughter or Steam Engine Technology of the Future: Fuel Cells Running on Alcoholic Cocktails, The Science Creative Quarterly, March 22, (2006).
30) Rose, L.: Boosting funding for clean energy technology, The Ubyssey, Friday, March 23rd, (2007).
31) Rose, L., Christie, M.: Science Creative Literacy Symposia, Combining Arts, Science, Engineering and Technology: http://www.youtube.com/user/UBCLTScom
32) Rose, L., Moll, R: Fuel Cells - Why bother, and When will they come? Presentations at various Professional Development workshops, for example, during the British Columbia Associations of Physics Teachers and Science Teachers (BCAPT/BCAScT) ProD Days 2007 and National Research Council Institute for Fuel Cell Innovation / Canadian Hydrogen and Fuel Cell Association (CFHCA) / Heliocentris Teacher ProD (2009). Presentation materials available on http://drfuelcell.com and http://admin.triumf.ca/docs/seminars/Sem20070421_Fuel_Cells.pdf
33) Spohr, H.V., Baghani, A.: Soap Bubble Physics Fun, published on http://ubclts.com/activityideas, BC, (2008).
34) The Science Teacher: Using the Overhead Projector to Demonstrate the Growth of Crystals From a Melt, pp.57-58, (1964)
35) Talesnick, I. (Ed.): Idea Bank Collation, A Handbook for Science Teachers Vol.1, S17 Science Supplies and Services Ontario, ON (1991) and The Crucible, Science Teacher Association of Ontario, ISSN 0381-8047, VIII(3), pp.25, (1977).

Acknowledgements: The authors gratefully acknowledge the professional aid with creating the content of this book from M.Ed. Jonathan Dale Sherman, National Education Specialists Scott Taylor, Sue McKee and Judy Wearing, as well as Hans-Otto Rose for an endless supply of crystallization experiments, and special needs educator Ingeborg Rose for handicraft and design ideas. Furthermore, Ruth and Lisa Solski from S&S Learning are acknowledged for editing and reviewing, Dan Day for illustrations, and Lise Pellerin for page layout and graphic design.

www.ingramcontent.com/pod-product-compliance
Lightning Source LLC
Chambersburg PA
CBHW080417250426
43670CB00052B/2870